Stephen Moore

POWER
and
CORRUPTION

The Rotten Core of
Government and Big Business

I would like to acknowledge all those, both in the United Kingdom and abroad, who assisted me in my endeavours, and give particular thanks to the Winston Churchill Memorial Trust. In Hong Kong, special thanks must go to Neil Parkinson, Ken Tso and Mike Squires; in Australia, thanks to Peter Darlaston, Frank Brown and Richard Laws. Eternal gratitude goes to Jenny Sanders, my long-suffering typist.

Contents

Dedicated with love to my mother, my father, Elaine, Stacey, Stephanie and Mathew.

INTRODUCTION

MOST CRIMINALS leave a trail. Perhaps a pattern will emerge during a spate of armed robberies, or a signature will reveal forged documents in a complex fraud. But corruption is a crime that thrives in the dark. It leaves nothing more than 'vapour trails' and there is usually little hard evidence for investigators to follow, only suspicion.

I have been fascinated by corruption for more than a decade and my interest has grown until it can justifiably be termed a passion. My direct involvement with corruption investigations has taught me that few crimes are harder to prosecute, such are the difficulties of following the vapour trail and proving offences have been committed. This is partly because corruption is a consensual crime, the effects of which are spread through the wider population. Neither the briber or the bribed will admit to their crime unless they fall out, or outrageous decisions are made which draw the attention of the police; even then, the difficulty of proving complicity in a court of law often means the guilty escape justice.

Corruption means that everyone suffers from increased taxes and missed business opportunities, yet few actually realise the causes - or are even aware they are being cheated. This book is, in some small way, an attempt to redress the balance, to help the public realise corruption is a crime directly affecting their lives. I and many other investigators believe that it is only when the public feel truly outraged that society will take a definite decision to prevent it.

But it is not only outright corruption which harms the worlds of business, politics and international commerce. Equally damaging is the atmosphere of distrust resulting from allegations of 'sleaze': self-enrichment, use of patronage, rule-bending and exploitation of office by politicians and public officials for private gain.

Many of the practices illustrated in this book are clearly illegal. Others, while legal, still attract public disapproval - and it is these extremes which set our parameters. In between illegal and sleazy are myriad shades of grey where boundaries of probity are difficult to define and where there is a blurring of public and private interests. Corruption is damaging democracy, but so to is the recent explosion of 'inappropriate' behaviour in public life: sadly sleaze is endemic in the Britain and numerous other political systems around the world.

Stephen Moore, 1997

1

CORRUPTION
IN
PARADISE

*"For de little stealin' dey gits you in jail soon or late. For de big stealin' dey
makes you emperor and puts you in de Hall o' Fame when you croaks."*
Eugene O'Neill, 'The Emperor Jones'

IT IS the sort of situation which would warrant the immediate despatch of James Bond 007 - an idyllic island in the Caribbean is taken over by a sinister criminal organisation.

In one of Ian Fleming's novels it would have been the evil organisation SPECTRE which seizes control. Bond would have despatched the villains with the help of a Walther PPK, a gorgeous girl on his arm and a vodka martini at the bar.

Yet the reality in the 1990s is just as dramatic.

The beautiful Caribbean island of Aruba, only five miles wide and 20 miles long, was 'bought' by elements of the Sicilian Mafia along with its 65,000 inhabitants. Everything of importance on the island was taken over by the mobsters, controlling elements of the police, politicians, customs and, most importantly, the banks. The 'ownership' of their own State offered wonderful opportunities for corruption on a previously unthinkable scale. Its very existence was founded on corruption and criminality.

Aruba lies just off the Venezuelan coast. During the age of discovery and conquest it was ignored by the Spanish, who described it as 'barren and useless', despite its beautiful long white beaches, and instead it fell into the hands of the Dutch and became part of the six Dutch Antilles.

Sleepy and ignored it was the perfect off-shore Shangri-La for the Mafia. For years they kept their ownership quiet, transforming Aruba into a staging post for cocaine smuggling. At the same time they bribed officials and used the island's banks to launder their money - channelling vast sums obtained from drugs, extortion, murder and prostitution across the world.

The authorities only discovered the Mafia's presence after a dramatic and violent police raid on offices in Caracas, the capital of Venezuela. Investigators seized computer disks concerning deals involving the Cuntreras family, one of the most dangerous Sicilian Mafia clans. The Cuntreras had been living in Venezuela for years and visiting Aruba for lengthy holidays. But the disks and other documents showed they had been doing more in the Caribbean than soaking up the sun.

The information seized by the police proved that more than 60% of businesses and economic life on Aruba was owned and controlled by the Mafia.

When the American authorities belatedly realised what was going on there was little they could do. One of their most expensive satellites was moved off course to 'sit' on top of the island and spot smugglers boats and cocaine drops in the ocean, but it was a difficult task even when the clouds allowed vision. One of the largest hauls of cocaine ever discovered in Britain came via Aruba.

Investigators came to the conclusion that the Mafia wanted Aruba not only to create the perfect base for corruption and crime, but also as a bolthole they could flee to when they needed to escape the law and avoid extradition to America, Europe or, more specifically, Italy.

Their fears soon seemed justified. In September 1992 Venezuela agreed to extradite back to Italy three of the most dangerous Cuntreras brothers: Guiseppe, Pasquale and Paulo, a trio known as the Black Emperors and reputedly worth more than $1 billion each, earned from drugs. Back home they were arrested and thrown into Italy's top-security Pianosa prison.

Investigators claim the Black Emperors took part in the appalling murder of Judge Giovanni Falcone, who was blown up shortly after he arranged for their extradition to Italy. They then assassinated Paulo Borsellino, Falcone's successor.

According to the US Drug Enforcement Agency the Cuntreras were the main force behind the acquisition of Aruba, a buying spree which started in the early 1980s, when the Black Emperors were frequent visitors to the island with their 'beautiful' wives. They stayed at first in Spartan accommodation, were kind to their kids and avoided ostentatious displays of wealth, according to locals. Meanwhile they were arranging the purchase of restaurants, banks, hotels, cafés, and every type of local business.

Organised crime was hardly a newcomer to the region. From the arrival of pirates and buccaneers centuries ago to the more recent arrivals of fugi-

3

tive financiers and money launderers, every criminal wants a home in the Caribbean. The island was quick to welcome the latest arrivals with their new investment and the Aruba government took little action, perhaps through fear of reprisals. Exceptionally, one member of the gang was arrested in 1988 and the Aruban authorities requested military assistance from Holland as protection. The Dutch took the request seriously and sent a frigate and a force of soldiers.

The Aruba experience shows that while the Mafia's global power has been under attack, the income from organised crime, the ability to hide it, to launder it and the ability to use it for corruption still poses great threats to international order.

Liberalisation of the world financial markets means that trillions of dollars criss-cross the world every day of the year, making effective supervision of the movement of black money impossible. The temptation to corrupt grows, and so do the means to corrupt.

The illegal drugs trade controlled by Mafia, Yakuza, Triad and South American drug cartels amounts to the financial resources of a large country. Politicians and law enforcement officers at all levels may be bought off with more money than they will see during an honest working life time. The organised crime cartels are hungry and ambitious for power, and they have the financial muscle to take what they want.

Aruba may be a small example of a corrupt state, but there are other, larger nations where corruption is a pervasive influence on everyday existence. Nigeria suffers more than most from an appalling international image created by its inability to deal with corruption and bribery. The front cover of one of the larger Nigerian magazines recently carried photographs of several forged British passports with the headline: "Why are we so corrupt?". It is not a difficult question to answer - Nigeria's problems stem from a fragile political system systematically undermined by the greed of those who seek to do business there.

Nigeria's infrastructure - oil, gas, telecommunications, electricity ports, and airlines - are all regarded as both inefficient and corrupt, and have been under investigation by special panels since 1994. Money simply seems to disappear.

An official report recently examined how the country's military rulers had managed to spend $12 billion of oil revenue between 1988 and 1994, money that had been placed in special project accounts to receive windfall receipts following the Gulf war. The money was allegedly spent in six years on what could neither be judged high priority nor regenerative investment. Throughout the developing world the whiff of corruption pervades - money which could be well spent on alleviating poverty or building an economic infrastructure is diverted to projects in which officials have a personal interest.

How the Evening Standard viewed the corruption problem in March 1994

TO DISCOVER the extent of corruption in Nigeria, I turned to Francesco, a tall, elegant Italian now living and working in London. Francesco, who asked that his surname be withheld, spent several years in Nigeria recently as the area manager of a large construction company, and wearily recalls his time in the country. "Corruption is absolutely, completely and utterly endemic in Nigeria. It is part of daily life, to the extent that you have to assume everyone getting a contract in the country is paying someone off," he said.

When Francesco first left Italy for Nigeria he was warned it was like another world. "It is a social and cultural shock. But it becomes a challenge. It becomes addictive because you just do not want to be beaten. But there is nothing you can do about it - I know the Far East and South America are pretty corrupt, but they are nothing like Nigeria."

Francesco's company was working on large projects - he has asked me not to be too specific - and would have to pay huge bribes to secure and maintain contracts. One of his closest colleagues was nominated as the bribe-payer: "he would meet one guy in the shade under a particular mango tree by the side of the road and give him a bag of money containing between three and four hundred thousand dollars."

A pay-off of that size is given only to the most senior figures. Francesco confirms the man taking the bribe was one of the country's most senior politicians. "This politician would take his cut, which was about half -

5

$200,000 - and then he would use the rest to pay off other people in his [political] party. It was a nightmare."

From the first moment that contracts were being planned, the price of corruption would have to be considered. Openly? "Bribes wouldn't be discussed in direct terms. But they were such a part of business life there were certain standards - people knew how much they could expect, and we knew how much we would have to pay them."

"If someone wasn't happy they would say they couldn't give us everything we wanted and there would be a bit of bartering. We would work out the costs and then calculate how much money would have to be used for bribes. Everyone was on the take. You give something to the architects, something to the politicians, something to the contractors, something to everyone."

"Sometimes more than 50% of a contract would go on bribes. Subcontractors would pay off the contractors. Contractors would pay off the politicians. Everyone was paying off everyone. Architects could do whatever they wanted, and appoint whoever they wanted. It was all based on the fact that a certain architect would know a particular military chief. It was all about personal influence."

"I know one architect, a friend of mine, who came up with a most noble way of getting a bribe. It was quite novel. He said there was a little statue, a Rodin, he had seen in London that he would like. And in that case his cut was the statue. Rather than dirty money he got the statue, worth about ₤15,000. For Western companies it can be difficult to disguise the bribes because the amounts are so large. Usually you just say they are 'commissions' to intermediaries who got you the contracts."

According to Francesco becoming corrupted is almost unavoidable. "Morality is relaxed because to survive people have to make money. To make that money you need to make a lot because making a little with their levels of inflation is pointless. Best of all you make foreign money. People wanted their money off-shore, and we would pay them straight into bank accounts in London or Switzerland."

"One rich Nigerian built a block of luxury flats in Lagos, and he would always ask what was in it for him. He would make contractors working for him pay for the privilege, partly in local money and partly in dollars into his foreign bank accounts. You have to understand that there is no way you can make money in Nigeria out of local money because it is a Mickey

Mouse currency, it means nothing, like roubles in Moscow."
He said corruption sears through every level of society. One government minister known to Francesco had all the money from Nigeria's
external oil revenues passing through his personal bank accounts. "It was
billions. He would say 'so what', because the money was just passing
through. But even if it only stayed there one day, it was earning vast sums
of interest. It was just the normal way of doing business."

"Anyone with any sort of political power or influence could expect
something in return. I was planning a trip back to Nigeria a few months ago
and asked a friend who was born there how I should go about fixing it
because he knows senior people. He would tell me this person had 'long
teeth', or that person had 'longer teeth', indicating how much money they
take, because they are like sharks. Everyone makes money that way."

Corruption was a constant presence. One time Francesco was leaving
the country and the flight was overbooked: "I was standing in the airport
queue and one guy pushed me from behind while my travellers cheques
and passport and everything were on the counter in front. I turned round
for a second and turned back and everything had been stolen. There were
thousands of people milling around - no chance of getting it back. I could-
n't face waiting, so I went to find Tiger."

Tiger is quite famous in Lagos. He is a one-legged old man who hobbles
around the airport on crutches - "one of three people at the airport who
you can use to get things sorted." When Francesco was there he was quite
old and semi-retired, but that was his life - hanging out at the airport and
helping people like Francesco to deal with and bribe the officials. He existed because of corruption.

"Tiger was 'our man'," said Francesco. "He worked for our company
and others. He was the best. Tiger was from the Yoruba, one of the three
main Nigerian tribes - half Muslim and half Christian. He used to dress in
traditional Yoruba dress with lots of colour and a tribal hat. Some of the
younger guys who did his job were not as good, and they would have problems. But not Tiger. He was like an old, cool cat. Whenever you had
problems at the airport, you should turn to Tiger."

Apparently it was a lucrative job. "He had lots of little guys working for
him who he would pay off, as well as the actual officials. Sometimes I would-
n't want officials to look through my bags because I would be bringing in
things like precision drills which you are supposed to declare because you

are importing things. Sometimes technicians would bring expensive equipment and samples, and I would ring from Italy and tell the company to get Tiger to help him through Customs. He would only have to pay the official - according to their level - a tip, perhaps less than a fiver [£5] to get us through."

Francesco returned to the incident when his passport and travellers cheques were stolen. "I asked Tiger if he could get me through customs without them. I told him my office would pay him. He gave me 20 Naira because I had no money left, and he took me over to passport control and told me to wait. He went to speak to someone and then told me to talk to someone else. I folded up the money and held it in my hand so it couldn't be seen. I went over to the guy, who was an official, and slipped it to him when I shook his hand. He smiled and waved me through.

"It is a nightmare for a new arrival. I know people who have arrived at the airport in Nigeria and said 'no way, I can't handle this', and they have left the country without even leaving the airport."

In the country itself, no-one was safe. "If the check-point police stop you, you would just give them money rather than have any hassles. They expected it and it was part of life. It was absolutely endemic. I would just give them a handful of Naira - perhaps £10. You could give them less if you were prepared to barter with them. But they would have guns and it can be incredibly threatening. The police would only want Nairas, medium people would want a combination of Naira and US dollars, and the top people would only want dollars. You always try to flog them Nairas first because the currency is worthless outside the country."

Francesco laughs as he remembers one rare occasion when one exceptional incident proved the rule. "I had a huge bag of money with me because I was going to pay off my workers. We were driving on the flyover into Lagos taking photos of the mosque. This car started following us. People inside were waving identification at us, but that means nothing because robbers pay soldiers and policemen to give them uniforms.

"I told the driver to get away because I thought they were crooks. They started chasing us and one was waving a gun, so we drove faster. They caught us at a roundabout.

"The police started beating up my driver and pushing me around. I had my camera on my chest and I told them I wasn't going to give it to them. They accused me of being a spy and took me to the Secret Service head-

8

quarters. On the way the traffic was terrible and we were stuck alongside an Italian colleague on his way to work. I shouted to him to raise the alarm because I was scared."

"They put me in an office and I thought they were going to beat the shit out of me. So I did what you always have to do, I tried to bribe them. I opened the bag containing all this money - perhaps £5,000 - and put it on the table. They were all young and earning a pittance but one of them told me to put it away. They were straight.

"I was amazed because normally when they are civilised and pleasant it is because they want money. Anyway, they let me make a phone call and I got one of the staff to bring down my passport. They confiscated it but let me go. In the end it only took a bottle of whisky to get the passport back.

"Lagos is such a crazy place that people are always being knocked over and you need a local driver. I would send mine from Abuja to Kaduna, which is about 200 miles, to pick up some batteries or take some drawings to an architect. He would give people a lift back and charge them. That is the normal thing, although he would completely deny it. It is like an entrepreneurial spirit.

"Nigerians are the merchants of West Africa. Even in past centuries they were the intermediaries in the slave trade. They were sending other Africans off to be slaves. They are very difficult to trade with - if you can get good deals in Lagos then you can get deals anywhere in the world. In general they are nice people but many are quite lazy. They do not like hard graft; perhaps that's why there is so much corruption there."

The political system is part of the problem, according to Francesco. "When the government changes or there were military problems then you have to bribe new people all over again just to re-negotiate the deals. They know they don't have long to make money because the political system is so fluid. There was one point where there were minor coups every six months.

"If you are a politician in Nigeria you have this feeling in the back of your mind that you are not going to be there for very long. And if you are in high office you have to milk the system while you can."

Francesco believes coping with sleaze in Nigeria becomes addictive. "When you have lived there so long you just can't live anywhere else. The danger is always present. Everyone has to get something."

For the more conscientious Westerners working in the country, there

9

are always moral questions about paying bribes. "Morally the problem was that you would see all these poor people on the streets who were literally dying. And then there were the richer Nigerians creaming off all this money in bribes."

"Although it is part of everyday life, people who go there are still a little embarrassed. You see all this money going into the pockets of people who do not need it. In a way you can understand the small amount of money going to an architect, for example, because that can be the only way they can get a bit of money put aside for a pension. But the big amounts would go to the local politicians, contract managers and officials. The politicians would appoint their own contract managers to look after a particular project. It is all a tricky thing, justifying bribery back in the West. People do not realise how much money is needed to oil the wheels."

"It is not surprising some British politicians have been accused of taking bribes. They are exactly the sort of people you have in Nigeria, who can put this person with that person or this company with that company. But it is particularly unforgivable in a country where people have a problem getting to the end of the week with enough food."

"What pissed me off was that it might be excusable if the bribery was to facilitate the building of a new irrigation system or to help the structure of the country, but it was mainly to build cathedrals in the desert: wasteful grandiose projects. I don't have any moral problems with it all now - but I did while I was there. It was nothing to do with the corruption and the bribery, it is more to do with the sheer wastefulness in Nigeria.

"There was one huge office building put up in Lagos where half of the technology only worked for two days. They had built it to be really hi-tech, but there is just no chance of maintaining it. Everything crumbles in Nigeria."

"The West is selling Nigeria stuff they do not need. What they need is help to advance their economy and society. But the West is exploiting the wider public with the connivance and help of the top people. Nigeria is a country where people have the latest Mercedes and the biggest TV's and the most modern video sets. And they still live in a iron hut. It is a very materialistic society. Labels matter.

"But the West flogs all their crap to Africa. We sold Nigeria Betamax videos, for example; the outmoded video format that lost out to VHS. They were the only ones who would take it. We are exploiting them, and clearing our consciences knowing we are giving them money back in bribes."

"It is disgusting, when you then see the social gap between rich and poor in Nigeria it is so vast. I remember one time when I was working on my site and one of the main sponsors of the project came to visit. The site was in the middle of a market - with all the smells and all these small huts. I remember he had a group of people, five or six, with him. They were all dressed in their finery and walked proudly round the market. Everyone stopped to look. When he came back into my building everyone followed him and stood outside. And then when he went back out to leave after our meeting, all these women were kneeling in front of him, kissing his hands and asking for money. It was like the Middle Ages."

So did democracy help? Francesco shakes his head cynically and sighs: "When it was a 'dictatorship' you only had to pay a few people, but when it became a democracy you had to pay off absolutely everyone."

LIZ SLY of the Chicago Tribune has studied the problem elsewhere in Africa. Under the headline: "Kenya no longer showcase of capitalism; Corruption fading Jewel of Africa", she documented the appalling experience of Tricia Washere, a 40-year-old single mother of seven.

Washere was one of a dozen poor families living in shacks on a small plot of land on the edge of the Nairobi district of Kayole. The morning before Sly arrived on her land, two truckloads of men had arrived with sledgehammers and guns, and had - quite literally - smashed Tricia's little house to pieces. Not content with the destruction of her home, they then proceeded to rip apart her furniture with axes and stole everything else that she owned, even her pots, pans and bed linen.

"I said, 'Let me take my things out first.' But they said 'no,' and then they stole my things," Washere told Sly. "I said, 'What about my children? They have nowhere else to live.' But they said, 'We don't care about your children; we have a job to do.'"

Their job was to evict all the families from the plot, and this they did with brutal force. One may ask why such suffering should be inflicted on 12 helpless families for the land had been occupied legally under a government-run program to help the poor. To the bemusement of those evicted, the thugs were acting on official orders. They had been hired for the day specifically to smash up the homes. They pulled out authorisation papers

11

from the city council, and they were supervised and watched by several armed and uniformed policemen.

Tricia had injured her hip three years previously when running away from a police 'swoop', and had sold porridge to construction workers and worked as a street trader, saving money when she could, in the hope the family could move into a more secure home. That dream was shattered abruptly when the thugs who smashed her hut also took her life's savings: 500 Kenyan shillings which she had hidden under a pillow.

With three of her seven young children around Washere, Sly gently asked what she would do next. In Sly's own words, Washere had recounted the details of her difficult life without emotion, "but now a big tear rolled down her cheek and her shoulders began to heave. 'I don't know,' she said, covering her face with her grubby pink apron to hide her despair from her children. 'I just don't know.'"

Sly is a tenacious reporter and asked John Kingori, Nairobi's Mayor for an explanation. Kingori blamed corruption for the violence, and said he had known nothing about it. One can imagine him shifting uncomfortably in his seat as Sly questioned further. "There is a group of powerful people, very high people, who are illegally getting plots of land for themselves or selling to others so that they can make money," he told her. "It's a very dangerous trend, and a very delicate issue, but it's happening all the time. This corruption is getting to be a very big problem, and it's getting very difficult to fight against it."

Kingori has apparently made a name for himself as an anti-corruption fighter but there is, in reality, little that even the mayor can do to stamp out the practice. "I fear it is too late," he admits. "This corruption has got into people's bones."

Sly believes that in certain African countries, characterised by high levels of state involvement in the economy and a high degree of authoritarianism, corruption has taken on destructive proportions. She is right. For those African nations which remain infamous for their appalling use of officially-sanctioned bribery are among the most troubled - Nigeria being the obvious example.

Kenya used to be a shining example to the rest of the Continent - a country of modern roads, soaring skyscrapers, 24-hour power and - always a good sign - an excellent sewage and drinking water system. But the 90s have seen a fundamental change. Corruption has bounded back. Nairobi has become a city of potholes, power cuts and street-beggars as corruption fills the pockets of the few at the top of the political ladder.

"Unfortunately, there is quite a bit of corruption, and it seems to be increasing," admits an official from the Kenyan Law Society with understatement. "Here, corruption affects government officials from the top to the lowest levels. It affects local authorities, it affects members of parliament, it affects judicial officers, it affects the police and it affects ordinary people. It seems to reach every layer of society and all kinds of people."

But, as ever, it is the top tier who are reaping the rewards. Scandals are frequent, and the most recent include an admission by the auditor general that $265 million has gone missing from the government's coffers - siphoned into the bank accounts of senior politicians.

Then there is the so-called Goldenberg affair, in which a small group of senior officials stand accused of stealing $250 million from the Kenyan Central Bank in 'compensation' for non-existent exports of precious stones and precious metals. So while the West and dozens of charities are doing their upmost to help the Kenyan economy, some of the country's leaders just laugh in their faces. $250 million is equivalent to more than half the aid Kenya receives in an entire year. In fact, it is almost as much aid as the USA gives to the whole of sub-Saharan Africa - 49 countries.

Unfortunately, few people outside Kenya hear of these scandals. Even fewer really care. Charities continue to campaign against poverty and injustice, such as that inflicted on poor Tricia Washere. Yet if only charities, international organisations and governments were to consider the effects of corruption on an economy such as Kenya they would realise that giving aid to such a corrupt nation is equivalent to filling a shopping bag with a hole in the bottom.

Chapter Two

A CRIME AS
OLD AS TIME

"The law locks up the man or woman, who steals the
goose from off the common. But lets the greater villain lose,
who steals the common from the goose."
Doggerel at the time of 18th century enclosures of common land.

I believe there is a dangerous complacency about corruption creeping into public life. Officials scoff at the idea of widespread or even occasional corruption, and in Britain there are those who argue that public sector corruption is not a problem. The statistical evidence for Britain, with an average of 100 reports per year entered in London's Metropolitan Police Corruption Index, would, on the face of it, support that view.

In addition, there is a definite and xenophobic belief that corruption is something decidedly un-British which begins at Calais. The British have placed great faith in the belief that their public institutions are corruption-free, even when faced with blatant examples of criminality. In passing sentence in May 1994 on Bernard Trevelyan, a corrupt Ministry of Defence official convicted of taking bribes, Judge Michael Harris said, "...we take pride that the public service in this country is largely free of corruption."

Even following the allegations of misconduct by MPs in the years that have followed, the Chairman of the House of Commons Public Accounts Committee felt able to say: "We are extraordinarily fortunate - there are, what, 184 countries in the UN. The number of them which have standards approaching ours are just a handful. We are a rare exception...".

But he is wrong. Those who would argue there is no corruption in the public service in Britain should consider other factors which probably make the UK uniquely susceptible to corruption. Britain has extremely strict libel laws; no Freedom of Information Act; little control over political fund-raising; lax regulation of the outside interests of Members of

14

Parliament; an ongoing large scale programme of privatisation of publicly owned assets; an aggressive arms sales policy and a largely unrecognised problem with drug-funded organised crime.

All these factors either provide opportunities ripe for corruption or hinder its exposure to public scrutiny. Public life in the United Kingdom is nowhere near as clean as many would have us believe - the temptations are simply too great.

The mechanisms to detect corruption do not exist in the United Kingdom: even before considering the problem of the consensual veil, drawn over events by the corrupt, there is a dangerous lack of transparency in public affairs.

Once evidence of corruption is actually sought, interesting facts emerge. The Poulson affair of the early 1970s is often cited as a landmark in the investigation and prosecution of corruption in the United Kingdom. The investigation snowballed from small beginnings until the number of public officials and businessmen requiring possible investigation reached 300, necessitating the issuing of an instruction that those in subordinate positions should not be pursued. No-one had the resources, or perhaps the will, to complete a clean sweep.

There are more modern examples if one only takes care to look. Monklands council in the Scottish region of Lanarkshire has been Labour Party-run since it was created in 1974. It is a depressing area founded on the combined strengths of the coal and steel industry both of which are long gone, leaving most of the locals struggling to survive in their small two-up, two-down council houses.

During the dying months of the last Conservative government, the Labour Party was forced to curb attacks on the questionable activities of some Tory MPs, and handle allegations of corruption levelled at their own supporters. In June 1996 Monklands council, which covers the towns of Coatbridge and Airdrie, was the subject of a report by Robert Black, a highly-respected Professor of Scottish Law. For nearly four years the council's leaders had been denying allegations of nepotism, political corruption, sectarianism and spending bias. Many of the allegations had been made by insiders who had grown tired of what they perceived as the exploitation of the public.

Black's report found the council guilty of most of the allegations against them. He discovered that councillors had allotted disproportionate funding for Catholic Coatbridge, rather than Protestant Airdrie. He found that 16 of the 17 councillors had a total of 68 relatives employed by the council. He found that a "suspiciously" high number of Labour Party activists had obtained jobs working for the council. He found that councillor's homes were always the ones repaired first by council workmen, and that work was undertaken on the houses on an "improper" basis.

It was political dynamite for a Conservative Party hammered by allegations of every possible type of sleaze, from influence-peddling and simple back-handers, to cash for prostitutes and bribes from arms-dealers. The Tories turned their guns on Labour.

But this was not corruption to shake the political pillars. Nobody died as a result. Monklands is not, after all, Lagos or Nairobi. Yet this is Britain, which is supposed to have checks and balances on the national and local political system. Surely, if such corruption can occur in a quiet area of Scotland, it can occur in the larger conurbations, where the award of a multi-million pound contract or an expensive planning order lies in the hands of a small number of councillors?

As with more serious allegations of corruption and large-scale vote manipulation in the Conservative borough of Westminster in central London (and other, smaller corruption scandals in Labour-run Lambeth in south London), the Monklands affair was the result of a system controlled by largely unopposed one-party rule. It did not come to light because Britain has enough checks and balances to prevent abuses of power. Until 1994, Monklands was the constituency of John Smith, leader of the Labour Party who tragically died that year. He was never remotely involved in any corruption but the whiff of a scandal locally threw the national spotlight on his local authority. That the issue ever came into the limelight was therefore something of a fluke.

OUTSIDE the United Kingdom, one means of piercing the consensual veil of corruption is the use of undercover law enforcement operations. In 1977 the Federal Bureau of Investigation in the USA created national and local sections concerned with organised crime and public corruption. This move was pre-empted in January 1976 by the formation of a public integrity section within the US Department of Justice, staffed by seven attorneys. By 1981 the number of attorneys had risen to 25 and between 1975 and 1985, the number of federal indictments for corruption charges increased almost four-fold to 1,182. Improving the mechanisms to detect corruption did not generate offences of corruption, the improvement simply led to more offences being uncovered.

In any environment with a lack of transparency in public affairs, two problems emerge. Firstly, corrupt practices go undetected. Secondly, practices which are not corrupt in law, even if ethically unsound, may appear to the public to be corrupt. The result is a public perception that something is not quite right, a feeling of unease. This vacuum is increasingly filled by the use of the word 'sleaze', helpfully defined (in an essay by academics Patrick Dunleavy and Stuart Weir) as "a populist word standing in for corruption and semi-corruption, or near corruption, in public life".

In this way, public bets are hedged; even if actions do not support an allegation of corruption, the apparent corruption is recognised. Sleaze is a word registering public disapproval for perceived abuse in public office within the established democracies of Europe and North America. Outside these established democracies, observers are happier to use the more explicit term 'corruption'.

If we attempt to define sleaze as corruption, near corruption, or unethical behaviour by those in public office, it would seem logical to attempt to define corruption. At its simplest, corruption has been defined as "the misuse of office for personal gain". However, even this short punchy definition warrants closer examination as accepted standards of morality differ according to geographical or temporal location. What would clearly be 'misuse of office' in twentieth century England, might not have been so in Tudor or Stuart times for example.

There is also a geographic difference, recognised by Lord Young, the former British Minister for Trade and Industry, speaking as Chairman of the Cable and Wireless telecommunications giant in May 1994: "The moral problem to me is simply jobs. Now when you're talking about kickbacks, you're talking about something that's illegal in this country and that, of course, you wouldn't dream of doing. I haven't even heard one case, in all my business life, of anybody in [the UK] doing things like that. But there are parts of the world I've been to where we all know it happens and if you want to be in business, you have to do [it].

"In many countries in the world, the only way in which money trickles down, is from the head of the country who owns everything. Now that's

17

not immoral or corrupt. It is very different from our practice. We must be very careful not to insist that our practices are followed everywhere in the world."

But if such actions are not 'immoral' or 'corrupt' why do they leave such a bad taste in the mouth and create a feeling of unease? Is the answer, when in Rome do as the Romans do? Or do we take the moral high ground? History is a good teacher. The norms of public life in sixteenth and seventeenth century England were very different to those today.

BEFORE the eighteenth century there was no clear line of demarcation between the actions of the ruler acting in his or her private capacity, and the ruler acting in a public capacity. Before this time, England was run as if it were a private concern with the ruler as proprietor. This is the theory of the proprietary state when all public offices are within the gift of the monarch to be sold, let or disposed of at will. The office holder's power derived from his noble status or favoured position at court rather than professional ability.

As the office holder's power was personal, in turn it was in his gift to sell off subordinate offices to the highest bidder and to generally function in such a manner as to maximise his own personal benefits. Such behaviour today would be seen as corrupt, but in the traditional period it was open to view and seen as perfectly legal. Power was devolved through a system openly based upon patronage.

It has been argued that the receipt of gifts and gratuities by government servants in the 16th and 17th centuries was not corrupt provided no harm was done to the state. Such gifts have been viewed as essential to the working of government when the Crown's revenue was too small to pay adequate official salaries for important positions. An interesting modern parallel may be seen in the views of those who argue that British Members of Parliament must be allowed outside interests to ensure that MPs of the right quality are retained by Parliament rather than lost to the lucrative world of commerce.

Given that there was great latitude in the payment of gratuities and the giving of gifts to public officials in Tudor and Stuart England, there were still acts performed by public officials which were censured as corrupt and tried before the courts. In the handling of revenues due to the Crown, the

line was clearly drawn and embezzlement of Crown funds was dealt with harshly.

In dealing with officers of the law, the line was never drawn so clearly as in the case of Francis Bacon, who became Lord Chancellor in 1618. Within three years, Bacon was arraigned for corruption for accepting bribes from litigants. In his defence, he said there were three kinds of gift which might be offered to a judge: bribes given in advance of a case in order to pervert the course of justice; presents given when the judge thought that the case was over when in fact it was not and still had some way to run; and presents given when the case really was over.

Bacon said that he was innocent in regard to the first type of gift, but confessed he might have inadvertently taken gifts believing a case had run its course, when in actual fact it had not. As to the third kind of gift, given after the case in question was completed, he freely admitted to taking such gifts which he thought was permissible. Bacon himself differentiated between gifts and the time of their giving. Indeed, there was a distinction to be drawn and there was a tightening of the definition of corruption through the centuries that followed. What was acceptable has become unacceptable. It may be that the 'sleaze' debate is the next step in the regulatory process - a further re-definition of corrupt practice.

The trial of Bacon highlights the difficulties of applying present standards to historical circumstance. However, while present judges would fear censure for accepting gifts from the winner in a legal contest, other public officials, having left public life, accept lucrative positions within private concerns with which they once worked closely, or even helped to regulate.

It would appear that in the judicial system, gratuities after the fact would attract suspicion that a "deal had been cut" and the system had been corrupted. But this would appear not to be the case for other public officials, including Government ministers, who shrug off any criticism and take-cover behind a shield of honour and self-regulating probity. No laws are broken, but public confidence is damaged.

Even in the somewhat lax environment of early 17th century England, the Secretary of State, Sir Robert Cecil, was fearful of accepting gifts of a certain value. He agonised over the acceptance of a gift of a coach and four horses given to him by the Earl of Northumberland, following his assistance to Northumberland in a profitable law suit. Sir Robert feared his assistance would be misinterpreted by both his enemies and Queen

Elizabeth I herself. Cecil wrestled with his demons and committed his fears to paper for all to later examine.

There is some inkling here as to what actually lay behind the corruption trials of the time. Cecil feared the Queen as his patron and his enemies. Acceptance of the wrong gift could be disastrous as it would provide enough ammunition for rivals to win the patron's ears, leading to a charge of corruption.

Sir Thomas More, Lord Chancellor to Henry VIII, was himself accused of corruption for accepting gifts from litigants (the practice of this time being to give a New Year present to friends and for litigants to give presents to judges). But it is interesting to note that these matters only became so grave as to warrant attention after More refused to accept Henry VIII as head of the Church of England.

MANY working in public life in the sixteenth and seventeenth centuries trod a careful line. Moral rules were judged against shifting standards. At one end of the scale, lesser beings in the royal court could not have survived without gratuities. At the other end of the scale, large sums were being made both from official and less than official means, under cover of the normal rewards for lesser officials.

By way of example, Sir Robert Cecil's yearly income from politics at his death, was £6,900, without any hidden income. In addition to this, he received a pension from Spain of £1,000 per annum from the year 1603, which was later increased to £1,500 per annum with a payment of £12,500 in 1607/8.

Furthermore, Francis Bacon's income as Lord Chancellor, before he was impeached, was the equivalent in today's terms, of at least £700,000 per year. In the light of such evidence, it is hard to believe that all public officials needed gifts and gratuities to provide incomes commensurate with their responsibilities. There were clearly acts which were as corrupt in the sixteenth and seventeenth century as they are now. Conversely, there were acts which were considered the norm and not viewed as corrupt, though they would be now.

The post of Lord Chancellor may be used to plot the course of mores in public life in England through the years. In 1718, Lord Macclesfield was appointed Lord Chancellor. Unlike Bacon, he did not accept bribes, but rather fell into the practice of 'selling offices'. Whenever he appointed a new Master in Chancery, he demanded an honorarium - as was the practice of the time. However Lord Macclesfield increased the price for offices to such an extent the Masters had to recover their investment by fair means or foul.

The easiest way of recouping such losses was for Masters to extract payments from litigants in Chancery cases, which they duly did. Cases were delayed and moneys extorted from the parties before legal matters were progressed. On occasion, Masters speculated with moneys held by them on trust on behalf of parties in Chancery. A speculative investment entered into by one Master involved the famous South Sea Bubble scandal and the truth came out in the ensuing financial collapse. The Lord Chancellor was impeached and fined £30,000 for his troubles.

Since Lord Macclesfield, no Lord Chancellor has been accused of accepting a bribe. However, examination of the actions of another Lord Chancellor in the 1850s provide an indication of the changes that have taken place in British politics.

Lord Cottenham was a shareholder in the Grand Junction Canal Company, which was in dispute with another party (Dimes v Grand Junction Canal, 1852). The company applied for an injunction which was granted by the Vice Chancellor and confirmed by Lord Cottenham on appeal without his disclosure of his interest in the company.

The House of Lords set the judgement aside. Lord Campbell said: "No one can suppose that Lord Cottenham would be in the remotest degree influenced by the interest that he had in this concern, but it is of the last importance that the maxim that no man is to be a judge in his own cause, should be held sacred... It will have a most salutary influence when it is known that in a case in which the Lord Chancellor of England had an interest, his decree was set aside."

A change is evident here. The political élite in sixteenth and seventeenth century England was a small group drawn from the Crown, principal courtiers and powerful aristocratic families. With the citizenry for the most part seen as 'mere sheep for the shearing', the exercise of power was not dependent on popular approval. This small, tight powerbase exercised nepotism, made decisions on the basis of bribery and generally misused office for personal or political ends, with the Crown seeking to draw upon divine authority for its actions. Policy issues and ideological differences

21

were largely absent from the arena and instead competition for private gain through patron - client relationships dominated.

So why did this change? The simple answer lies in industrialisation, where the wealth generated slowly forced the aristocracy out of its favoured positions close to the Crown. The Crown's need for revenue and its desire for the support of commercial élites led to wealth becoming a path to office, undermining the traditional aristocratic domination of political life. This movement gathered pace during the Industrial Revolution and the broadening of the franchise with the electoral Reform Acts of the 19th century.

With the wider participation in the political process in the eighteenth century, a process which gathered pace in the nineteenth century, power centres diversified and the proprietary state withered on the vine. It could be said that corruption in the modern sense was a Victorian notion which followed this greater participation in politics and the need for popular assent to the actions of those in public life.

In 1853 an Act was introduced which ended patronage in the Civil Service. Entrance to the service was to be by competitive examination, the aim being to make the resultant Civil Service neutral in colour and unbiased. The 1883 Corrupt and Illegal Practices Bill limited the amounts that could be expended upon election expenses. The 1888 Local Government Act made provision for 62 new elected County Councils and with the later enfranchisement of women, popular government had arrived.

If this historical model is correct, democracy should lead to a reduction in corrupt practice: the wider the political arena, the greater the chance of public sanctions which must offer hope to developing nations. How then do we explain the current tide of 'sleaze' which is enveloping the democracies across the globe, and in particular the Mother of Parliaments in London?

Many countries in the developing world may be likened to the pre-democratic times of Western Europe. The pressures to misuse office are, in many ways, the same.

Many commentators attempt to demonstrate that corruption in developing nations is a continuation of traditional gift-giving practices, where the subservient pay tribute to the élite as a sign of allegiance. At given times of the year, usually religious festivals, the wealthy would make gifts to the poor. Symbolic continuation of such traditional practice may be seen in Britain each Maundy Thursday when the Sovereign gives specially-minted 'Maundy money' to selected elderly men and women. Such a quaint custom, however, goes little way to explaining bribes of millions of dollars involved in procurement in the third world.

Within societies where family and community groups are strong, ties within such units are strong. In young nations they are often stronger than loyalty to the state. The first obligation in such societies is to the family, community or ethnic group, with the state often seen as an amorphous, impersonal entity. The government servant in such a state faces a great moral dilemma - there is a gap between the standard of behaviour expected of a public servant and the popular values held within that society which are supposed to propel him or her towards favouring his community or ethnic group.

The gap is particularly noticeable in former colonies of the Western powers, where standards were imported and imposed upon the native population in a 'Mother knows best' style, while traditional order was still very much in existence. Small wonder that in many of the younger nation states traditional group loyalties remain firmly entrenched.

In a similar way we have already seen that in Tudor and Stuart England there were many examples when personal enrichment or benefit to a clique or political élite were pursued rather than the best interests of the state and its citizens. This is the crucial moment when human nature confronts a weak political and legal structure.

With this desire for personal enrichment through powerful cliques goes a requirement for entrepreneurs and business people to protect themselves and their ventures. This can be difficult in a state system where the rule of law lacks consistency and legal requirements can change according to the whim of a small number of the governing élite. Under such circumstances, office holders are able to extort money from the business class, while at the same time this class is eager to buy itself the protection denied to it through a weak legal system.

In another way, the exclusion of certain groups from a society may make these groups more prone to use bribes to obtain influence. The means employed to gain influence will change according to the nature of the excluded group. A large organised group may resort to violence, or a coup, to achieve its ends. However a small number of excluded people with plenty of money may use their wealth to 'buy' into society on a smaller scale. Political donations given in the expectation of honours are often an attempt to buy legitimacy. Perhaps this could be termed the 'barrow boy made good' school of capitalism - wealth buying what birth and upbringing denied.

An example of excluded groups using differing methods to achieve influence can be found in Ghana in 1960, when Nkrumah's Convention People's Party provided favoured access to a new, lower middle class. Many wealthy Ghanaian traders, professionals, bureaucratic élites and foreign companies were removed from the previous positions of influence they held under the previous colonial system.

Certain community groups such as the Ashanti and the Tiv were similarly penalised by the new regime. Two methods of adjustment were used: many of the smaller but wealthy groups, such as foreign companies and traders, used bribes, including giving contributions to the CPP, while the Ashanti and the Tiv regions became areas of unrest and public disorder. Those regions lacked financial muscle, but contained enough people to make physical opposition a threat in their attempt to restore access to the decision making process.

We must also appreciate the role of government in developing nations. If political parties, trade unions, business interests and other political power groups are weak or underdeveloped, then government is not subject to checks and balances. If a state is subject to a dictatorship, then it follows that potential opposition - political or economic - will be suppressed.

In many former colonial states where democracy was left behind by the imperial power, it was a process destined to struggle because it was a structure imposed by edict. The traditional societies lacked, for the most part, the educational base to encourage wider political participation and the commercial classes hungry for representation and political influence.

A small political élite does not make for democracy, whether it be in seventeenth century England, or a modern developing nation.

The problem is exacerbated in developing nations in that democracy may be smothered at birth. Democracy imposed without the economic and educational base becomes power concentrated in an élite, who run the state as a proprietary concern. The demand for 'grease money' may reach such a level that increasing industrialisation suffers and is slowed, economic growth is damaged and educational programmes are stunted as foreign investors withdraw.

24

A Crime as Old as Time

Most military regimes seizing power in Africa and Asia quote corruption in the former civilian governments as their reason for seizing power. But imposed parliamentary democracy often produced weak leaders serving the narrow interests of their own ethnic or tribal groups. Without effective opposition founded on a bedrock of an educated electorate and participating interest groups, democracy simply cannot work.

A theory has been propounded here, that much of what we would call sleaze or corruption in developing nations is simply a staging point on the journey to democracy. It is a means of exerting influence where no formal political channel exists. Where then does the feeling of unease come from once we have explained corrupt behaviour or sleaze in this way? The answer is twofold: once democracy has been achieved and formal channels for influence exist, corrupt practice offers an illegal advantage and damages a system of which we approve. Secondly, where the behaviour occurs in a developing country which does not have the firm democratic base to reflect interests, it is seen as undermining a system which the west hopes will be achieved.

If we accept these arguments we must ask why in our western democracies do we now have this problem of 'sleaze'? The simple answer is that it is seen to undermine a system of which we approve. Explaining how the problem has reached such a level within our democratic societies will take a little longer.

ONE MUST ask whether the 'sleaze' debate has been precipitated by a new view of practices long accepted as normal politics, or whether the blame is to be laid at the door of privatisation programmes, career politicians without outside sources of income and the materialism born in the 1980s.

Those living in western democracies live in an age where few feel secure in their chosen workplace. The drive for economy, efficiency, 'delayering' and 'empowerment' of staff has sapped confidence. Levels of responsibility are pushed down to a minimum. Layers of supervision are being removed, leading to reductions in controls.

This climate of engendered insecurity is coupled with greater opportunity to abuse new found responsibilities and a loosening of the bonds of loyalty to the employing organisation. Following the 1987 British general election, the introduction of market-testing, internal markets, compulsory

25

competitive tendering and the devolution of budgets were all measures intended to herald great change in the public services and increasing involvement of the private sector in areas once the sole preserve of the public sector.

The Audit Commission and the Public Accounts Committee have recognised the delegation of financial and managerial responsibility in the public sector has increased the likelihood of fraud and corruption. The greater the number of sources available to meet public sector demand, the greater the temptation for private sector supplier to indulge in dubious practice. After all, they argue, "we have to secure contracts in a intensely competitive market place." The mirror view lies with public servants feeling insecure yet overloaded with few ties of loyalty to their service, and salaries which are inferior to those in the private sector.

The same financial reasons which are removing layers of middle management in Britain are providing opportunities for insecure public employees to loot the public purse. In addition, compulsory contracting out in local government and the new Private Finance Initiative has produced deals for which it could be worth becoming corrupt.

But the problem is not confined to the United Kingdom among all the western democracies. At a time when the country faces record unemployment and harsh public spending cuts, Wolfgang Schaupensteiner, a Frankfurt lawyer seen as Germany's top anti-corruption prosecutor, believes "economic crime has spiralled to levels never believed possible until a few years ago. We are witnessing a loss of values in Germany. Moral and ethical principles in German boardrooms have gone to the dogs. Crimes are committed daily and the only thing that seems to matter is profits and selfish materialism."

Schaupensteiner has spent years warning economic crime and public sector corruption has been rising in Germany. Since 1987 he has prosecuted 1,624 cases of bribery and secured more than 300 convictions. In one of the largest corruption scandals ever to have surfaced in Germany, Schaupensteiner is investigating a group of Frankfurt officers and companies suspected of corruptly obtaining millions during the building of a new terminal at Frankfurt airport. In a country which prides itself on honesty and teutonic efficiency, and amid rising unemployment and deepening insecurity, something has gone seriously wrong.

In response, the government of Helmut Kohl has made the fight against

A Crime as Old as Time

An anti-corruption department in Hong Kong spreads its message by commissioning a television drama series. These are some of the stars.

corruption a priority, preparing measures that include the raising of the maximum prison sentence for corruption in the public service from 5 to 10 years. Yet the term 'Politikverdrossenheit' has entered the German language. A literal translation is an apathy towards politics and the term is used to describe a sense of malaise in German politics and a public feeling of disillusionment. The established parties in Germany: CDU/CSU, the FDP and SPD, are all widely viewed as self-serving and populated with politicians whose primary role is self-enrichment through the acquisition of privileges and financial rewards.

Similar feelings are found in Britain. Rather than seen as a vocation for public service, political post-holding is widely seen as primarily a means for enrichment. This theory is reinforced by the genesis of the career politician who increasingly dominates parliament. Whereas politicians were previously drawn from the ranks of the professions, trade unionists, teachers or university lecturers, it is more likely now that a Member of Parliament will have been previously employed in a position to provide a bridge to a parliamentary seat. If this seat were to be lost, there would be no profession to return to. The only alternative under these circumstances is to make hay while the sun shines and prepare a financial nest-egg for life after parliament. A public suffering from job insecurity is highly likely to view such feather-bedding of politicians as sleazy. Non-executive board positions where large sums are paid for just a few hours work merely serve

27

to rub salt into the wounds of a 'downsized' public.

During the privatisation of public utilities, the sums paid to outside consultancies linked to politicians engendered a public feeling that 'jobs for the boys' is the rule of the day. The salaries paid to those at the top of the tree in former public-sector industries just serve to reinforce the negative public opinion.

Increasingly in the United Kingdom and the Western democracies, a political career is seen as a rapid way of improving social and financial position, especially with the growth of political and business interaction. There is opportunity here for those with a knowledge of both worlds to straddle the gap. Men, and to a lesser extent women, move easily in either the political or business sphere. These intermediaries pay their way into the party with their ability to provide inside knowledge or expertise using confidential information and close personal contacts.

If politics is the way for the ambitious to pursue a lucrative career, then power is the obvious first step. But this requires money. The race for political contributions again provides opportunity for those who criticise the political system. All political contributions, notably those that may be sourced to foreign origins, beg greater questioning. At the very best, when there are financial pressures, greed sometimes overcomes good judgement. At worst the source of the contribution matters not, only that it was made in the first place.

Here lies the trouble: the border between actions the public finds distasteful, and actions which are clearly corrupt and criminal. The allegation may be made pejoratively that a government has been 'bought' by its political contributors, but in some areas of the world, the expression 'bought' does not refer merely to exerting some influence, but to the setting of political and economic agendas.

Chapter Three

GLOBAL
WARNING
.

"Government even in its best state is but a necessary evil;
in its worst state an intolerable one." Thomas Paine

W ANG JIANYE paid heavily for falling prey to temptation in Communist-controlled China. The former planning chief of Shenzhen, a booming economic area close to the border with Hong Kong, was accused of taking $900,000 in bribes, and keeping a mistress. With two others who were accused of fraud, Wang was paraded through the Shenzhen streets on the back of a lorry, surrounded by grim-looking soldiers. The lorry then drove into the local sports stadium where a crowd of 5,000 was waiting.

Wang's crimes were read out over the loudspeaker, a gun was put to his head and he was shot dead, as were the two other prisoners. A member of the local disciplinary commission said Wang deserved his fate because he was 'an obstacle to the progress of the economy'.

Wang Jianye and two other victims await their execution in a Chinese sports stadium

29

The incident in 1996 shows that corruption is perceived as a problem in the most strictly regulated countries. The Chinese clamp-down on corruption has been mirrored in Communist Vietnam where leaders have declared war on corruption because, they said, it exposes a flank for enemies to 'sabotage the revolution'.

Phom Huy Phuoc, director of the Tamexco import/export company, was tried with eighteen others for embezzling or wasting more than £30 million. Phuoc himself was accused of pocketing £16 million. As the 'war' progressed 4,900 separate cases of corruption were brought to light during the six-month period to September 1996. Ta Huu Thanh, chief state inspector, admitted: "They don't show the real situation." The real situation was even worse.

The countries of the Former Soviet Union are also struggling to curb a decline in the standards of public administration. It is alleged in Russia that the Mafia has links with the highest ranks of politician and civil servants, but this is nothing new. As in China, corruption was a problem in the Communist era and has only become more obvious.

In Bulgaria in January 1997, two weeks of street protests with people demanding immediate elections led to the Socialist Party publicly apologising for two years of misrule and corruption. The party announced the start of an operation to root out corruption as a result of which many scandals have come to light.

IT MAY JUST be understandable that corruption flourishes in countries where there is an absence of democracy, or where it is a fragile flower. In more accountable regimes it can have enormous political implications, as many recent scandals demonstrate.

In India, the world's largest democracy, bribery and maladministration is headline news. Within the Congress Party, which has ruled the country for all but four years since independence, such allegations have reached the highest level. In 1996, the Prime Minister, P.V. Narasimha Rao, was himself implicated, and forced to announce that no MP's involved in such wrong-doing would be accepted as candidates in the forthcoming general election. It then emerged that friends, wives and relatives would stand in the place of those deselected.

Controversially, one of Rao's sons was to stand in the election, while another son was alleged to be involved in a sugar scam. Rao led the Congress Party into the election under a cloud, with disastrous electoral results. Rao resigned the leadership and was later indicted on three corruption charges, each carrying a possible seven year jail sentence.

According to police sources, more than 20% of candidates for an election in Uttar Pradesh had been involved in serious crime including bribery.

IN JAPAN, a shining example of virtue and efficiency to many in Europe and North America, corruption is, alas, ever present in the public sector. A senior bureaucrat in the Health and Welfare Ministry resigned recently over allegations he received £350,000 and other gifts including a car from a nursing home developer. The bureaucrat was accused of receiving the gift to obtain approval and subsidies to build old peoples homes in Tokyo.

The country was shocked at the seniority of the civil servant involved, but Japanese bureaucrats have extensive powers and are particularly susceptible to corrupt relationships with businessmen. Indeed corruption has been a problem for several decades as a recent book by Jacob Schlesinger, a former Tokyo correspondent for the Wall Street Journal, shows.

He tells how a small corrupt group of politicians came to dominate Japan's ruling Liberal Democratic Party (LDP) after the Second World War, buying support and buying off the opposition with dirty money. The most accomplished exponent was Kakuei Tanaka who became premier. In the mid-1970s he took a junior colleague home to teach him his modus operandi. He picked up a cardboard box from a number in his office and emptied a pile of money onto the table. "You can't be a politician if this amount of money makes you nervous," he said.

He went on to explain the etiquette of 'palm-oiling'; acting humble, bowing deeply and offering the backhander at a time when it is difficult to refuse. He suggested money could be deliberately lost at mah-jong, or it could be offered as condolence money if someone had lost a relative.

Tanaka was later embroiled in a huge bribery scandal involving the American plane-maker Lockheed, and he was forced to resign as premier. However he kept his seat in parliament with huge support, and carried on where he had left off. In a final irony, he had himself elected to the parliamentary ethics committee.

31

Power and Corruption

THE DAMAGE inflicted on the Asian 'Tiger' economies by bribery has been acknowledged by Chuon Leekpai, a former Prime Minister of Thailand. He has admitted high levels of corruption have damaged the public's faith in government. One administration, which Leekpai opposed, fell from office amid such allegations. Several European embassies had issued a public complaint about the award of a lucrative contract to a local company which had submitted a higher tender than foreign competitors.

Perhaps the greatest Asian corruption scandals can be found in South Korea, where two former Presidents have been convicted of receiving huge bribes from industry while still in office and fined a total of $610 million. A dozen former Presidential aides and nine businessmen were also found guilty of bribery.

Among the businessmen convicted were the chairman of Samsung and the founder of Daewoo. Daewoo, Korea's fourth-largest company, allegedly gave a $6.5 million bribe to win a contract to construct a submarine base. President Roh Tae Woo allegedly threatened to give the contract to another company unless Daewoo paid the bribe.

Several years ago, Gulf Oil sacked its chairman after it was revealed he had a $12 million slush fund which he used to pay-off the Korean President. Even one of the most prominent opposition leaders has admitted accepting nearly $3 million from President Roh's slush fund for one recent Presidential campaign. Many readers may find this peculiar. So did the Korean public when the deal was revealed. Kim Dae Jung, the opposition leader, tried to explain his acceptance of the money by claiming that apart from the limited public money available for the campaign, there was virtually no other way for his party to raise the funds.

It is said Roh amassed a personal slush fund of $653 million from bribes and 'forced donations' from business and industrial leaders. South Korea was agog when Roh was arrested - the first time a South Korean President had been held by the police. It is easy to see how Roh amassed his wealth. The price for obtaining a licence to start a bank was apparently between $2 million and $4 million; golf course licences went for more than $7 million, a reflection of the nation's obsession with the sport.

But part of the reason for the public outrage directed at Roh was not simply because he had amassed such a sum, but because he appears to have been incredibly selfish. Some former Presidents had been careful to spread the money around to keep their friends and supporters happy.

An example is former President Chun Doo Hwan (Roh's predecessor). His followers fondly recall the time Chun distributed 50,000 envelopes of money to his major supporters and gave his retiring chief aide a present of more than $400,000 so the astonished man could start up his own legal business. When Chun resigned from office, he even handed his massive slush fund over to Roh for him to use. "He was an old-fashioned paternalistic politician," said one Korean expert approvingly.

The most famous example of his power involves one of Korea's largest conglomerates, the Kukje Group. Kukje had won a contract to build a country-club - a lucrative business in Korea - but the firm virtually collapsed overnight when Chun decided to cut off all their lending. Officials, even from within the Government, have since admitted it was in retaliation to the paucity of the Kukje Group's political donations. One of Chun's aides allegedly told the chairman of Kukje: "Don't you think you should say thank you?". Kukje's response was clearly inadequate.

EMERGING markets in the countries of Central and South America are suffering just as much, as an example from Brazil shows. In July 1994, the American company Raytheon won a contract to supply a complex radar system to the Brazilian government to provide surveillance of 'the Green Hell', a local nickname for the Amazon jungle.

The $1.4 billion project involved 20 ground-based radar stations, eight airborne radars, 10 weather radars, a satellite and more than 200 monitoring stations to keep an electronic eye on a land mass greater than half that of the continental United States, and looking for illegal farming, mining, drug trafficking, and illegal logging.

President Clinton had lobbied hard to win the contract for the US firm as 20,000 'job-years' were on the line. He had written to the Brazilian President and US Commerce Secretary Ron Brown (who later died in a plane crash in the former Yugoslavia) visited the country accompanied by Dennis Picard, the Raytheon chief executive. Further oiling the wheels was the US Export-Import Bank which approved one of its largest-ever loans to Brazil, $1.3 billion.

The main opposition was a French company, Thomson CSF, who had plenty of experience of working in 'difficult climates'. The CIA said Thomson had allegedly offered bribes to officials to support the French

33

bid for the contract. The allegation was leaked to the press and led to an investigation by the Brazilian Congress.

Three months after the bribery allegations, ESCA, the Brazilian contractors on the project, were removed amid further allegations of corruption, for allegedly attempting to defraud a government department. Because of a furore which followed the demise of ESCA, groups opposing the very concept of the project persuaded a judge to invalidate the entire contract.

Then came a hammer blow to the Americans. Someone (fingers were pointed at the French secret service) taped telephone conversations allegedly made between a Raytheon representative in Brazil and a presidential aide. Jose Alfonso Assumpcao, who worked for Raytheon but not as an actual employee, was recorded saying: "That son-of-a-bitch Gilberto Miranda [a member of the Brazilian Senate] is really trying to cause problems, disrupting everything. He doesn't want the project to come through. He's creating difficulties." "Damn," said Julio Cesar Gomes dos Santos, the presidential aide. "Did you already pay this guy?... He's disrupting everything, creating difficulties," said Assumpcao.

The presidential aide never actually responded directly to the bribery question. But it was still enough to fill pages in the Brazilian press. Alexandre Barros, one of Brazil's top political consultants, said that what fascinated and appalled the public was the casual manner it was discussed: "People were surprised by the bluntness of what was said. When you read 'so-and-so is a son-of-a-bitch' and 'have you paid this guy?' it is explosive." Everyone involved subsequently denied that any bribes were paid and claimed the tapes had been doctored to give a distorted image of the conversation.

But it was too late. The whole debate over the surveillance system was reopened. The Brazilian Senate opened a new inquiry and a group of independent public prosecutors called for an investigation into corruption, bribery, "influence-peddling", threats of violence and espionage.

Fernando Collor de Mello, the President, had only recently resigned amid charges of accepting money from those wanting to influence policy. The fall-out from the 'Green Hell affair' led to three other Brazilian government ministers resigning and Brazil's most respected newspaper declaring it all an 'insult to the nation'.

While reluctant to comment on the corruption claims directly, a spokeswoman for Raytheon in the US admitted the twists and turns in the contract

- which one observer likened to those in the Amazon itself - had been 'unprecedented'. "I'd heard people say you have to have a lot of patience with overseas contracts," she said. "They always take longer than you think they will."

She might also have commented on the role of the French and US secret services, which were pressed into action to help win the contract for the two competing companies. In such circumstances, no-one plays on a level playing field.

CENTRAL AMERICA has fared little better. The Mexican Congress voted to set up a commission to investigate the financial background of Raul Salinas, the brother of the former President, following allegations he had been involved in the assassination of a former political leader, J Ruiz Massieu. Salinas was jailed, after it was revealed that he held 44 bank accounts for his secret earnings.

No-one was surprised. Business visitors, tourists and locals speak of traffic policemen who harass drivers, invent a minor offence, and then rip up the penalty ticket in exchange for a miserable handful of pesos. Forbes Magazine has said there are only three countries with more billionaires than Mexico. A small group has become fantastically wealthy while the less privileged sink further into abject poverty. Mexicans know almost anyone in the country can be bought - from the most senior politician to the lowliest public official.

According to investigators the majority of corruption cases in Mexico are linked to the ruling Institutional Revolutionary Party (the PRI), which has controlled every aspect of Mexican life for several decades. Corruption has gone beyond pay-offs and bribes for financial gain . Many question whether the political system could survive without corrupt politicians using bribery and blackmail to play factions off against each other.

Two rebels from the left-wing Popular Revolutionary Army (the EPR) - which has been waging an insurgent campaign against the government - were recently found to have close links to that government. Several independent campaigners, who questioned whether the PRI had been providing financial backing for the EPR in a bizarre bid to show strength in the face of armed opposition, were subjected to death-threats.

One senior Mexican Congressman, quoted anonymously, said corruption was now an integral part of life in the country. "It no longer offends the public," said the anonymous Congressman. "It is the most democratic thing in our system."

MIAMI, Florida, 'the Sunshine State', is equally troubled and may have picked up many bad habits from its Latin American neighbours. The economic fallout was recently a $70 million budget deficit with the city teetering on the brink of bankruptcy.

Several state judges were been charged with taking payoffs to acquit guilty gangsters. Senior officials have grown wealthy without having any visible source of income, yet the difficulties of proving guilt mean local and federal investigators have been unable to get charges to stick. One mayor has been tried and acquitted three separate times on charges of corruption and extortion, and then been re-elected.

"They are just laughing in our faces," said one senior FBI agent. "We have municipal officials with vast homes and several cars which they claim they have bought on their meagre salaries. We know they're lying. They know we know they're lying. But until someone breaks ranks and confesses to giving a pay-off we can't take them down." US Attorney Kendall Coffey, the federal government's top prosecutor in the city, recently resigned after he was caught in the Lipstik night-club, where he had bought a $900 magnum of Dom Perignon with his American Express Gold card. As a dancer hired by Coffey stripped off her bra and fondled herself in front of him, he allegedly sank his teeth into her arm. Coffey later claimed he was depressed after he lost a major drugs trial.

The FBI launched Operation Greenpalm, an attempt to catch some of the most corrupt officials in the city. Three city officials have been charged with extortion, corruption and embezzlement, and a county commissioner - a senior position - was caught on tape discussing how he would take a $300,000 cut from a $600,000 fee for a financial bond deal.

The Feds arrived in force when the Unisys Corporation complained to federal investigators that Manohar Surana, the city finance director, allegedly asked for $2 million to help the company win a $20 million computer contract with the city. The investigation widened and eventually caught the city manager, Cesar Odio. He resigned when accused of trying to take $12,500 a month from Cigna Healthcare, Miami's insurance compa-

ny, which was to be shared with a Miami political lobbyist.

As if that wasn't enough for the city of 'Miami Vice', another senior politician was caught by the FBI demanding a $200,000 cut of the Unisys contract. A pressure group has been formed with the stated intention of abolishing the city government and letting the local county authority take over.

IN EUROPE there are just as few clean regimes. Politicians, political parties, businesses and even governments have fallen as an active media uncovered stunning examples of questionable behaviour.

In France, the Bouygues construction group, which employs 70,000 people and owns the television station, TF1, was caught up in allegations of corruption. Chairman of TF1, Patrick Le Lay, and the group chairman, Martin Bouygues, were accused of misuse of corporate funds by diverting funds to a fictitious consultancy.

The French press speculated that this money was used to fund French political parties. In the late 1980s and early 1990s, it was commonplace for large French firms to make secret donations to political parties, but strict legislation was later adopted to prevent this.

Just a month later it was announced that Jean Tiberi, the Mayor of Paris and political ally of President Jacques Chirac, had been placed under formal legal investigation, along with his wife, on suspicion of misusing public funds. But this was just the latest stage in a legal and media investigation that had begun in 1994 when an investigating magistrate, Eric Halphen, was appointed to examine the accounts of companies dealing with City Hall in Paris.

Prior to his election as President in 1995, Chirac had been mayor for seventeen years. Allegations of kickbacks and clandestine party funding were made to Halphen, but proof was lacking with witnesses later retracting their statements.

Then in May 1996 Francois Ciolina, former head of the public housing office in Paris, offered to give evidence alleging it was common practice for building contractors to present inflated bills for payment, some of this money being directed to the funding of the Neo-Gaullist Rassemblement Pour la Republique (RPR) Party. The allegations seriously damaged the reputation of Chirac but Ciolina also alleged that the son of Jean Tiberi,

Chirac's replacement as Mayor of Paris, had been allocated a council flat in Paris ahead of others on the waiting list.

The flat was allegedly refurbished at a cost of £200,000 to the taxpayers with the fitting of marble flooring, sound-proofing around the lift shaft and three paint jobs to achieve the desired shade of pink. Tiberi denied that favouritism had been shown and the Paris Prosecutor ordered no further investigation of the case.

Then in June 1996, Eric Halphen, the investigating magistrate, executed a search warrant at the home of Jean Tiberi, and seized a number of files. Among the papers was evidence that the Mayor's wife, Xaviere, had been paid more than £25,000 for the production of a report for a local authority, run by a fellow Gaullist mayor and friend of the Tiberi family. The 36 page document was alleged to be riddled with spelling mistakes, devoid of useful comment and plagiarised. It formed the focus for the formal legal investigation announced in March 1997. Despite this, Tiberi held his seat as Gaullist MP for the fashionable Latin Quarter with commentators putting his remarkable political survival down to the public's tolerance of political chicanery. However, that may not be the whole story. Allegations of vote-rigging are now being investigated.

FORMER SPANISH Prime Minister, Felipe Gonzalez, has not escaped censure. He was accused of ensuring his brother in law's company was awarded a $112 million contract to construct a nuclear-proof bunker beneath the prime minister's home and offices in Madrid. The Prime Minister denied he had taken advantage of his official position.

At the time, three government ministers had already resigned: two for failing to tackle corruption and another for alleged tax evasion. In addition, the country's former chief law enforcement officer, Luis Roldan, was a fugitive from Spanish justice accused of enriching himself by manipulating lucrative contracts to modernise barracks of the Civil Guard.

Roldan, the first non-military head of the 75,000 strong paramilitary security force, had been seen as a possible interior minister before details of his fortune with ensuing allegations were made public in 1993. Before fleeing Spain, Roldan had threatened to reveal information to compromise the Spanish government. "If I go to jail," he said, "I won't go alone."

Roldan dropped numerous hints about secret slush funds before being

detained in 1995 in Laos and jailed on corruption charges. Later that year brought further accusations that Siemens, the German electronics company, had paid $20 million in bribes to Spanish politicians and public officials, including Luis Roldan, in connection with a $1.3 billion rail contract. Siemens denied the charges of corruption, but confirmed it had contracts with consulting firms which, it later transpired, were also involved in the Filesa scandal, an affair involving a network of companies providing illegal political funding.

EVEN SWITZERLAND has seen standards declining. In August 1995, a Zurich court sentenced a disgraced local government official to five years imprisonment for accepting bribes amounting to $1.2 million. Four Zurich businessmen were also sentenced to suspended prison sentences. Raphael Huber was in charge of restaurant permits in the Swiss canton of Zurich and allegedly used his ill-gotten gains to build up a beautiful vineyard estate in Tuscany, northern Italy, complete with ornamental lake.

Following exposure of the scandal Huber stayed in Italy to avoid Swiss justice. According to the state prosecutor, a 'reign of fear' had been established with Huber accepting payment in the form of loans, or encouraging businessmen to purchase paintings by his deceased father at inflated prices.

Other investigations in Switzerland have focused on government auditors who are suspected of bribery for favouring government suppliers. Other officials are alleged to have taken bribes for the issue of false vehicle documents for second-hand car exports to Africa.

PERHAPS the last word should go to Italy, land of the Cosa Nostra. Corruption is an ever-present problem - a factor in the failure of almost every Italian Government in the last fifty years.

One scandal with the most far-reaching repercussions has involved the helicopter company, Agusta, which was accused of paying large bribes to ensure that its machines were purchased by the Belgian Government. As the scandal came to light, an air force general committed suicide and a number of government ministers resigned. Several years later, the Belgian economics minister at the time of the deal, Willy Claes, was forced to quit his post as the head of NATO, the North Atlantic Treaty Organisation.

In another instance, Carlo de Benedetti, President of computer compa-

39

ny Olivetti, admitted paying £5 million in bribes to win contracts for the company. The 58-year-old financier - Italy's third richest man at the time - was sentenced to a six year prison term for bribing politicians to secure lucrative contracts from the public sector, including one from the Italian Post Office.

Benedetti surrendered himself to the magistrate investigating the case, and openly admitted that he was forced to pay-off corrupt politicians and executives from the Post Office to win the contracts, "otherwise they would have given them to someone else who offered them more money, that is just the way things work".

"I gave in to the politicians only when I found it necessary to consider the survival of my company and its tens of thousand of employees," he insisted.

A spokesperson for Olivetti was equally unrepentant, saying the company was 'compelled' to pay the bribes: "We could not avoid them on some occasions. There were other times when Olivetti refused to pay."

In **Zaire,** the toppling of President Mobutu Sese Seko of Zaire by the rebel Alliance of Democratic Forces for the Liberation of Congo-Zaire led by Laurent Kabila in May 1997 ended a 32-year regime characterised by the coining of the word 'Kleptocracy' to describe the rapacious nature of its leaders. During his time in power, President Mobutu amassed a fortune which peaked during the mid-1980s at an estimated £2.4 billion with at least 20 properties in ten countries worth an estimated £23 million.

Mobutu's fortune is alleged to have been derived from a number of sources. Zaire has big reserves of copper, cobalt and diamonds, and a Belgian intelligence report claimed Mobutu had diverted £1 billion over a ten year period from state-owned 'natural resource' companies. Other analysts estimated that Mobutu and his associates diverted up to 20% of the state operating budget for their personal use.

Another source of income alleged to have been exploited by Mobutu was Western business interests seeking opportunities in Zaire. As a result, stories of grand corruption in Zaire were legion with the resultant imbalances in the system caused by such misconduct; for example, the country actually contracted for the supply of equipment for more airports than the country operates.

Foreign aid was seen by President Mobutu's regime as fair game. Of the $8.5 billion of foreign aid received by Zaire during the period 1972-1997 much was never used for the intended purposes. The problem was adeptly summarised in an International Monetary Fund report of 1982: "The President's bureau makes no distinction between state expenditure and personal expenditure."

A number of **Zimbabwean** government ministers were accused of diverting money for their own benefit from a compensation fund intended to compensate veterans of the war of independence. More than 70,000 people applied for payments from the £22.5 million fund, though only 35,000 fighters against white rule were registered when independence was achieved in 1980. One of the three independent MPs in the Zimbabwean parliament, Margaret Dongo, was thwarted by the actions of Zanu-PK loyalists, after calling for an examination of the payments but not before Dongo had listed 46 senior figures in government including Cabinet ministers who she alleged had received payments of Z$850,000 (£46,000) from the fund. Dongo, speaking in Parliament in April 1997, said: "There are so many Cabinet members, army officers and police officers who are claiming funds for serious disabilities, it is a wonder the Government can function at all."

The veterans fund scandal was only one of several gripping Zimbabwe at the time. Having struggled with the government for two years to set up a cellular telephone network, the country's most successful black businessman Strive Masiyiwa lost out on an American firm represented by Zanu-PK supporters including Leo Mugabe, the President's nephew. Leo Mugabe also represented the little known Cypriot firm which won a £50 million contract to build the new international airport in Harare.

The President of **Gabon,** Omar Bongo, cancelled a visit to France in April 1997 amid allegations he had benefited from an international fraud involving the operations of the French oil company ELF in his country. ELF imports 16% of its oil from Gabon and there had long been allegations that much of the oil revenue was distributed among the Presidential entourage.

As a result of allegations made, André Tarallo, a close friend of French President Jacques Chirac, and the chairman of ELF's subsidiary company in Gabon, was held in temporary custody before being allowed out on bail of approximately £1 million. Tarallo, who supervises ELF's affairs in a number of African states allegedly controlled an account holding millions of pounds for the benefit of himself and others including President Bongo. Even before these allegations were levelled, Bongo had made protests to Chirac following a French request to block an account held in the British Virgin Islands containing funds allegedly deposited by the President of Gabon. Bongo's reaction to developments was to threaten sanctions against French oil interests in his country.

Amid predictions of a sharp rise in corruption in **Hong Kong** after the return of the colony to China, John Wood, the first director of the Serious Fraud Office (SFO), and a former Director of Public Prosecutions in Hong Kong, reportedly returned to the territory to help combat sleaze and public corruption. Wood had been appointed as a consultant to Lee and Allen - a forensic accountancy practice. Wood was quoted as saying: "It is extremely difficult to predict, but I think the general view is that corruption will increase because of the influence of China."

In May 1997, **Brazil** was rocked by scandal when it was alleged that five Congressmen had accepted money in return for votes allowing the President, Fernando Henrique Cardoso, to stand for re-election. In a taped telephone conversation one senior politician spoke of receiving £118,000 for his vote. Few voters were surprised by the allegations, in a country where vote-rigging at local and national elections is commonplace.

Between 50 and 80% of the cocaine reaching Western and Central Europe is supplied via the **Caribbean** basin, with increasing evidence that senior figures in government and business are involved in the trade, which is plied among the 1,200 or so islands in the region. A report on Aruba by a Dutch commission states: "The island has fallen prey to powerful families that not only dominate its economy but use Aruba to benefit South American drug cartels ... and use the government as errand boys." Sandro Calvani, head of the United Nations Drug Control Programme's Caribbean office in Barbados reinforces this view with his stated belief that drug barons are becoming involved in political affairs to further money laundering and drug trafficking aims. In Calvani's words they are: "trying to short-circuit the democratic process."

In the **Balkans** in May 1997 Marko, the son of President Milosevic of Serbia, opened the country's newest night-club, called 'The Madonna', in Pozarevac, the Milosevic's home town. The only television coverage of this inauspicious event was on a television channel controlled by the President's wife. Some observers noted that before five years of civil war wrecked the country, the Milosevic's lived in a small two room flat; by the end of the war, they had a villa in central Belgrade, another villa and yacht in Greece, and property in Pozarevac.

The experiences of President Tudjman of Croatia (dubbed 'the richest man in central Europe') were similar. Tudjman's son Stjepan supplied the army with food and clothing while his daughter Nevanka, nicknamed 'Madame Mercedes', took over a department store and duty-free shops at Croatia's airports and border crossings.

Abdala Bucaram, the President of **Ecuador** for six months before he was thrown out of office in early 1997 after huge public demonstrations, allegedly presided over a regime riddled with corruption. Bucaram, known as 'El Loco' (the madman) because of his outrageous behaviour - such as dancing with semi-naked woman, and recording a CD with a rock group - was declared 'mentally incapable of governing' by the national Congress. It was only after Bucaram had fled to Panama that it was alleged he had been plundering the national reserves. His son, Jacobo, who was in effective control of the state customs service, allegedly diverted container loads of goods for his own use. Bucaram threw a huge party for his son at the end of 1996, and it is alleged the country paid the extortionate bill. In Congress, the President's brother, Santiago, somehow managed to find the money to employ 80 assistants on huge salaries.

In spite of the allegations of theft and fraud, the interim government which replaced Bucaram concentrated on trying to extradite him from Panama on charges of treason for his criticisms of the military. Opposition politicians believe they were trying to divert attention from continuing corruption in the country.

Binyamin Netanyahu, the **Israeli** Prime Minister, faced repeated calls for his resignation in April 1997, despite the Attorney-General's decision not to lay charges against him, as recommended by police, in connection with a scandal over a public appointment. While ruling out criminal charges, the Attorney-General Elyakim Rubinstein said the Prime Minister's conduct 'raised puzzling questions' with evidence that gave rise to 'suspicion that there were other considerations' relating to the appointment. That have been said, speaking on behalf of state prosecutors, Rubinstein added: "But we don't think this can be proved beyond a reasonable doubt."

The scandal had broken in January 1997 when an Israeli television journalist claimed the short-lived appointment of a little known lawyer as Attorney-General - Roni Bar-On, had been made as a result of a deal whereby Aryeh Deri, the leader of the ultra-Orthodox Shas Party who was facing corruption charges, would be granted a plea bargain by Bar-On. Deri's importance to the Netanyahu government lay in the ten seats controlled by his party within the coalition. In exchange for favourable treatment, it was alleged that Deri had offered to persuade his ministers to support proposals to pull Israeli troops out of the town of Hebron.

Netanyahu admitted making a mistake in appointing Bar-On, but stressed that prosecutors had vindicated him of any criminal act. He promised that in an effort to avoid such mistakes in the future a ministerial committee would supervise future governmental appointments. Netanyahu promised 'our government will be more open and sensitive'.

The allegations made against Aryeh Deri provided the backdrop for a further scandal for the government: in August 1996, the Israeli Justice Minister Jaacov Neeman had resigned after being accused of attempting to influence a witness in the case against Deri. Neeman was finally cleared by a Tel Aviv court of perjury and obstructing justice in May 1997.

Chapter Four

WAR
CHESTS

*"Money distorts democracy. It is like ants in the kitchen. You need to block
up all the holes and keep the money out."*
Democrat Senator Bill Bradley (New Jersey) during the
1996 US Presidential campaign.

Have you booked the TV advertising campaign? Organised the
posters and leaflets? Arranged the newspaper ads? Modern political campaigns involve vast sums of money, and their mushrooming
costs are leading politicians into potentially compromising situations.

Money they receive for their campaigns may not go directly into their
own pockets, but the acceptance of campaign donations can be just as
damaging if there is even a vague suspicion of a quid pro quo. A lack of
openness and transparency as to the identity of donors adds further fuel
to the flames of suspicion.

Complex US electoral rules on party funding and donations are a legacy
of the Watergate affair of the 1970s. Companies are not permitted to make
direct donations to candidates, but there are ways to exploit weaknesses
in the system. In the United Kingdom, direct donations to parties are still
legal, although the 1985 Companies Act requires corporations to disclose
any direct and indirect political expenditure in company accounts.

The focus on political funding in the United Kingdom was sharpened
by a House of Commons Home Affairs Committee report published in 1994
with the title 'The Funding of Political Parties.' This report resulted from a
number of disclosures which proved embarrassing to the Conservative
Party during the period 1992-3. Donations allegedly had come from John
Latsis, a Greek shipping tycoon, from Y. K. Po, a Hong Kong businessman,
and an illegal donation of £440,000 had been made by Asil Nadir, the fugitive Cypriot businessman. The illegality surrounding Nadir's donation lay

in the fact that while it was made using a company cheque, the donation was never declared in the company accounts. It was then revealed that Octav Botnar, the former head of Nissan UK, had made large donations to the Conservative Party using an offshore bank account in Jersey. Botnar, like Nadir, is currently wanted in the UK regarding a big alleged tax fraud.

When it came to the reporting stage, the Home Affairs Committee (which had an inbuilt Conservative majority) saw little need for change; certainly not change which would have led to the publication of names of donors providing large donations to political parties. It was felt that no case had been made for the state funding of political parties: "We see no reason why parties which have little public support should be either financially dependant on the taxpayer or be able, unjustifiably, to undermine the income of those who enjoy that support." In addition, there was felt to be no need to place a limit on the amount of money which a party can spend during an election campaign.

But who gains in this fund-raising free-for-all? Conservative Party accounts for the year ending March 1992, the run up to the 1992 British General Election, showed an income of £23.5 million. A surprising £16 million of this money could not be traced by scrutineers from outside the party.

The Labour Party, who were then in opposition, had an income in 1992 of £16.6 million. Of this, £8.5 million came from trade union affiliation fees, £1.6 million from membership subscriptions and £4.9 million from fund-raising. The Labour Party has expressed a willingness to publish the source of donations over £5,000, whether required by legislation or not.

In 1992 the Liberal Democrats total income was only £3 million, of which 35% came from membership subscriptions and 61% from donations. The party was willing to publish information about donations if the Home Affairs Committee decided that the rules should be changed to require this.

Of the small parties, the Green Party declared the largest donation they had received was £100,000 and in common with Scottish Nationalist Party, recommended disclosure of donations over certain levels: £5,000 by the Greens, £20,000 favoured by SNP. Plaid Cymru, the Welsh nationalist party, believed that "controls should be placed over the sources of finance of political parties". In the same period the Ulster Unionists disclosed an income of only £116,000.

In October 1996 Robin Cook, who was then the opposition - or 'Shadow'

- Foreign Secretary, announced that a Labour Government would outlaw the acceptance of foreign donations by parties in the United Kingdom, would force parties to declare the source of donations in excess of £5,000, would require companies to hold ballots of shareholders before making political donations and give shareholders the right to opt out of their share of a political fund.

In anticipation of such legislation, Cook announced the Labour Party would disclose the identity of donors making donations in excess of £5,000, challenging the Tory party to do the same: "Three years ago, the party was bankrupt with an overdraft of £19 million," he said before the 1997 general election. "Today that party boasts a £20 million surplus to buy its way back to power with saturation advertising. The public is entitled to know who is bankrolling the campaign."

These are certainly interesting times for political fund-raising in the United Kingdom and the 1990s have witnessed big changes in the way the two major parties, Conservative and Labour, secure funding. British companies have deserted the Conservative Party en masse since the 1992 election. Many leading companies have severed links with the party, and the amount contributed by the FT-SE 100 leading companies has fallen from £1.4 million in 1991 to £760,000 in 1995, according to Pensions and Investment Research Consultants, a research firm. The feeling among many United Kingdom companies that the Conservative Party has betrayed them, coupled with controversy surrounding party funding, has led many to withdraw from the arena.

But the party also faces pressure from institutional investors in the city. A growing number of fund managers - who can each control millions of shares - would like to see an end to political donations made by companies in which they hold an interest. A former donor to the Conservative Party, Legal and General, which made a donation of £30,000 in 1995, has become disenchanted with government policy. Norwich Union, which owns shares in many donor companies has said it will vote against company boards seeking 'blanket' approval for donations and was likely to vote against all donations.

The irony is that while their traditional sources of funding desert the Conservative Party, the Labour Party is tapping into these same sources. When Paul Blagborough became head of the Labour Party's finances in August 1993 he took on the task of redefining how the party would raise its funds. He saw that as the traditional power of the unions - historically the financial backbone of the Labour Party - within the party was reduced, they would become reluctant to provide the millions of pounds made available when union influence within the party was at its zenith.

Blagborough realised that one way of weaning the Labour Party off reliance on union donations was to pursue other big donors. The first strategy used was to approach 'personalities' in the arts and entertainment field, the 'luvvies' as the Conservative Party disparagingly calls them. But when Tony Blair took over the leadership of the Labour Party in 1994 it became apparent he was seeking the financial support of business too.

Approaches were made through business forums and city breakfasts, and the initiative worked. During 1995, Pearsons and Tate & Lyle, both traditional donors to the Tory party, gave £25,000 and £7,500 respectively to its arch enemy. At least 17 donors gave more than £5,000 to Labour in 1995, the largest corporate donor (£1m) being GLC Ltd, run by Laurence Staden, a dedicated socialist. Others backing 'New Labour' included Paul Hamlyn, the multi millionaire publisher; Philip Jeffrey, whose fortune lay in the Fads DIY chain; and Geoffrey Robinson, businessman and Labour MP for Coventry North West.

A £1 million donation was made to the Labour cause in 1996 by Matthew Harding, owner of the insurance group Benfield, who was later killed in a helicopter accident. Harding denied he was seeking tax breaks for his company or trying to curry political favour: "What New Labour under Tony Blair's leadership is trying to do with the country is the right thing at the right time. In the United States, you can be fabulously wealthy and a Democrat and nobody bats an eyelid."

Harding's support was by far the largest personal donation to the Labour Party to date and Labour politicians made much of the party's willingness to divulge the identities of its financial backers, and challenged the Tories to do the same. In September 1996 Tony Blair proudly stated in a television interview that unions contributed less than half of the Labour Party's income. Delighted with the Harding donation, Labour hinted at other big donations to follow.

Much has been made of the reversal in Tory fortunes from a £20 million overdraft in 1992 to solvency, as announced by party Chairman Brian Mawhinney at the Conservative Spring 1996 conference. Following Matthew Harding's donation to Labour, Mawhinney remained adamant the

Conservatives would not divulge names of donors: "It is up to the donors to decide if they want publicity. It is a matter for Mr Harding how he spends his money and who he tells about it. The truth is only a millionaire could afford a Labour government."

By way of further counter-attack, the Tories claimed that Labour, far from being open about its funding, covers up much of its union support. There may be some truth in these allegations, but I have investigated both methods of funding, and believe far more attention should be paid to the secretive and Byzantine world of Conservative Party fund-raising which allowed such an astonishing turnaround in party fortunes in four years.

The authorised version of this financial miracle is simple. Under the direction of Lord Harris of Peckham, the deputy treasurer, the party has obtained funds from self-made entrepreneurs who expanded their fortunes under 17 years of Tory government. Harris himself, starting from humble origins, became one of the party's strongest financial supporters after building a carpet business yielding him a personal fortune worth an estimated £128 million. The new donors also include Eddy Healey, property and DIY interests who gave £50,000 in 1995; Paul Sykes, property, "tens of thousands"; Sir John Hall, chairman of Newcastle United Football Club, property, £100,000 plus; and Tony Gallagher, construction, £114,000.

Conscious of controversy surrounding donations from Asil Nadir and Octav Botnar, Lord Harris played down the amount of foreign money received by the Tory Party. The official line was that only 10-15% came from overseas, amounting to £2-3 million.

The Conservative Party, however, faced further allegations of 'sleaze' in May 1996, when the Secret Intelligence Service (MI6) allegedly discovered that the Conservative Party had received tens of thousands of pounds from donors linked to the Bosnian Serb leader, Radovan Karadzic, a man accused of war crimes. The revelation that money was being paid to the Conservative Party while British troops were performing peace-keeping duties in the former Yugoslavia renewed calls to ban foreign donations to British political parties. John Major, the Prime Minister and leader of the Conservative Party, denied Serbian donations posed a threat to British soldiers and rejected calls for an investigation by Parliament's Nolan Committee into party funding. Tony Blair, leader of the opposition responded: "When money is accepted from foreigners, most people in this country would think ... that the best thing would be to have the Nolan Committee consider party funding, so that justice could be done and be seen to be done and not covered up and hidden by the Conservative Party."

Tory fund-raising attracted further attention in late 1996 with reports that the Inland Revenue was making enquiries into the business affairs of Wafic Said, a Syrian born businessman and Tory donor. In 1995, he said in a letter to a financial magazine that he had donated less than £300,000 to the Conservative Party and averaged £20,000 per year since the Tories came to power.

But Said had first come to public attention in 1992 during a Commons enquiry into the Iraqi 'supergun' affair, when he was named as the agent responsible for brokering defence contracts with Saudi Arabia worth £20 billion - a deal known as 'Al-Yamamah'. Said admits a role in the process but rejects the 'arms dealer' tag attached to him.

Given the withdrawal of many corporate donors, the Conservative Party has not been slow to exploit every fund-raising opportunity available. Party treasurers encourage wealthy entrepreneurs to make large interest free loans to the party on the grounds of tax efficiency. Top rate taxpayers would pay 40% tax on interest earned by their money on deposit. However if the money is loaned to the Conservative Party, advantages accrue. Firstly, if paid into an account in overdraft, the interest charges are reduced in the party's favour. Secondly, if paid into an interest bearing account, due to the party's special taxation status, all interest earned would be tax free and payable to the party. The party has held peculiar tax status for a long time and this was last confirmed during a case against the Inland Revenue in 1992 when it was successfully argued party funds were controlled by the leader and therefore corporation tax was not due.

If loans made to the party are repaid within a single financial year, the loan does not have to be disclosed in the party's annual accounts. On the other hand, loans are repayable at 48 hours notice which gives the donor control over its money, but also leads to a 'Sword of Damocles' situation which gives a donor awesome influence within the party. The threat of withdrawal, it is justly claimed, can lead to an unethical abuse of influence.

In an effort to dispel the belief that anybody was going to get a free lunch out of a political fund raising the Tory party founded The Premier Club. The Club offered government ministers as after-dinner speakers to businessmen supporting the party. In return, the businessmen paid up to £100,000 for the opportunity to meet the ministers. The patron of the club,

*"I'm afraid the After Eights
are another £10,000"*

From The Times, July 1996

as the name implies, was John Major. Also on offer as well as lunches and dinners were an information service and the opportunity for detailed briefings on government policy. According to a club brochure, all activities were kept 'strictly private and confidential'.

"This is the most blatant example of financial corruption in the history of even this sleazy government," said Robin Cook, the Shadow Foreign Secretary. "Businessmen shouldn't be allowed to buy access to ministers or influence on policy by slipping a secret bung to the Conservative Party."

There have been further damaging claims that Frances Penn, the Premier Club secretary, who worked in the Conservative Central Offices treasury department, advised would-be donors how to conceal donations by listing them in company accounts as 'entertainment'. This allegation was flatly denied but the whole saga led inevitably to further demands for Conservative Party accounts to be opened to independent scrutiny.

Both Robin Cook and Liberal Democrat leader, Paddy Ashdown, also highlighted the role played by the Premier Club chairman, property millionaire John Beckwith. Beckwith was a player in a group of companies bidding for a £1.5 billion government contract to buy 58,000 military homes. Robin Cook called for Beckwith to be removed from tendering for the contract stating: "there is a flat conflict of interest between raising money for the Tory Party and making money from the Tory government." In a letter to John Major, Paddy Ashdown said Beckwith's involvement would "cause justifiable public apprehension of sleaze... the whole process as described is dubious and democratically offensive."

Fund-raising clubs such as this are highly successful in the United States, where they operate in a different political climate. Because of various Federal laws, the names of contributors are published, thus reducing controversy and avoiding the appearance of improper behaviour.

But is Labour any better? Tony Blair has made great play of the fact that union funding now accounts for less than 50% of Labour Party income. However, this is only true if the Party's special election fund is excluded. Otherwise unions contribute over half the party's income through affiliation fees and even more through donations.

Union funding of the Labour Party, and indeed Tony Blair's personal office, works through a number of channels. A special 10 pence levy on 3.3 million trade union members raises £330,000, which is passed to the National Trade Union/Labour Party Fund established in 1995 by union leaders. Of this £330,000, £180,000 is used to help pay for Tony Blair's 15 strong staff. However the money is routed through Labour's general fund which allows Blair's office to deny it receives union money directly. This is true, but only technically.

Labour has a separate general election fund administered from John Smith House and run by trustees who include the general secretaries of leading trade unions. More than 80% of the £4.5 million pounds in the fund at the end of 1995 had been donated by unions. This money has its origins in the £2 annual political levy paid by union members, of which 75p is used for the general election fund. By the second half of 1996, the fund stood at £7 million with plans for a donation of a further £1 million from the 'Victory Appeal Fund' of affiliated trades unions.

During the course of 1996, the Labour Party abandoned direct trade union sponsorship of about 150 MPs and set up new arrangements for the payment of money. Blair believes the new arrangements will reduce payment direct to a sponsored MP. Additionally, by limiting election donations to MPs to less than 25% of the total expended by the MP, he or she can avoid having to record their union role in the House of Commons register. The unions can pay up to £5,000 each to each of 150 constituencies and this money is not recorded in Labour's national accounts.

The Transport and General Workers Union has, however, refused to make payment to constituency parties in place of the payments formerly made to 30 sponsored MPs, who included Blair and other senior Labour MPs. Left-wingers within the union favour a system whereby those MPs who speak strongly in favour of the union are paid more.

Whereas members of the Shadow Cabinet have previously received union payments for researchers and office facilities, these monies are now paid from a centralised trust called the Labour Frontbench Research Fund.

It is estimated the unions have contributed £100,000 to this fund in the period 1995-96. The organisation of the fund is such that recipients are prevented from seeing where the money they receive actually originates.

In view of the above, it would appear that Blair's attempts to free the Labour Party from allegations of union influence through union bankrolling have not yet succeeded. Where he has had some success is in camouflaging these important sources of finance.

AMERICAN electoral rules on party funding and donations have their roots in the Watergate Affair of the 1970s and a desire for electoral probity. However, such is the nature and cost of modern electioneering that, where loopholes exist, they will be exploited. The US elections of November 1996 revealed examples which are likely to haunt President Clinton into and throughout his second term of office. Appealing to a campaign audience in Virginia, Ross Perot, the maverick third force in US politics during both the 1992 and 1996 Presidential elections, asked the poignant question: "Is it responsible and in the best interests of our country to have a President who has the next two years of his life facing Watergate 2?"

Clinton and his wife Hillary face further enquiries relating to the Whitewater affair involving the bankrupt Madison Guaranty bank and the Clinton's role in the Whitewater investment. Kenneth Starr, special counsel in the case, has subpoenaed Hillary Clinton to testify before a grand jury. More relevant to the subject matter in hand, Starr is examining the theory that Whitewater was used as an illegal campaign slush fund for Clinton, who was Governor of Arkansas at the time. In addition to the Whitewater affair, allegations over political donations continue to dog the President.

The rules for contributing to US election war chests may be put simply. Companies are not permitted to make direct donations to candidates but can contribute by two methods. Firstly, companies can constitute Political Action Committees (PAC's) with funds raised through an optional levy on employees wages. Employees normally elect a committee which decides the candidates who will benefit from donations. Corporate PAC's are limited to making a maximum donation of $5,000 to individual candidates for each election.

Secondly, money donated to the party as opposed to individual candidates is described as 'soft money' and can be donated directly from company funds. Restrictions on soft money funding are not clearly defined and such donations have risen relentlessly. Election law forbids foreign companies to make contributions though American subsidiaries of foreign companies may do so. Similarly, contributions from foreigners not resident in the USA are also illegal..

Corporate funding has become integral to the US political system as each party attempts to build a larger political fund to ensure it cannot be out-spent by its rival. From the other side of the fence, companies spend ever increasing sums on the political parties so as not to be outdone by business rivals or special interest groups opposed to the company's sphere of activity.

As is well known, tobacco companies are desperate to combat the influence of the anti-smoking lobby and have donated approximately $20 million over the past decade to political campaigning. The level of spending has more than doubled since 1993 to counter increased activity in favour of anti-smoking objectives. In a similar vein, oil and gas companies have spent $20 million attempting to combat a harder line in environmental legislation and threats of a tax on energy.

While corporations will explain the benefits of political donations in terms of access to politicians rather than undue influence, suspicion will always remain that it is the latter which motivates donors. However, the scandals of the 1996 Presidential campaign revolve around foreign donations, and donors with links to organised crime. These emerged when the Democrats returned a $20,000 donation to a convicted Miami cocaine smuggler, Jorge Cabrera. He had made the gift in November 1995 and was arrested two months later after a raid by law enforcement officers revealed a cache of nearly 2,700 kilos of cocaine.

In view of the relatively small sum involved, it is possible to have some sympathy with the recipients when one considers the amount of money donated to the two major US parties. "You can't do a background check on everyone who gives you a campaign contribution…," said Leon Panetta, the White House chief of staff.

However the attention paid to this donation and the attendance of a Russian businessman, Grigory Loutchansky at a Clinton fund-raising dinner was magnified by publicity relating to Asian donations. For the record, Loutchansky has been described by Time magazine as 'the most pernicious unindicted criminal in the world'. Loutchansky was turned away from a second Clinton fund raising event when the Democratic Party learned that his Vienna-based company, Nordex, had originally been funded by the KGB and was suspected of involvement in the acquisition of nuclear materials by North Korea and Iran.

The Asian dimension attracted much attention. Within days of Clinton's re-election, the Democratic Party decided to return a contribution of $350,000 to an Indian businessman based in the USA when it was learned he could not pay creditors and had no assets in the US. The suspicion was that he was merely acting as a front man for funds from foreign interests.

There is a lot to be suspicious about. Investigators have discovered that when Vice President Al Gore spoke at a Buddhist temple, the monks - who had taken vows of poverty - were able to find $140,000 to contribute to the Democrats. Each donor wrote a personal cheque for $5,000, the limit for individual contributions. Bizarrely, it is feared the temple may have been used as a front to launder money.

Then there was John Huang. One of the busiest fund-raisers for the Democrats during the 1996 election campaign, Huang, a former Taiwanese air force officer who was born in China, later joined the Hong Kong Chinese Bank, owned by the Indonesian Lippo Group, and in the mid 1980s moved to Little Rock, Arkansas, where he helped to establish a new operational base for Lippo.

During his time in Little Rock, Huang got to know Bill and Hillary Clinton well. In 1994, Huang left as President of the Lippo Group USA to join the Clinton campaign and was given top secret security clearance, apparently on the personal instructions of Ron Brown, the commerce secretary. According to several sources, Huang was not subjected to the background checks normally required for a person born in a foreign country. Suspicion is growing in Washington that Brown, who was killed in a plane crash over Bosnia in 1996, ran the commerce department as a clearing house where political favours were traded for funds.

Huang maintained close ties with his former boss at Lippo, Mochtar Riady. His son, James Riady, lived legally in the US in 1991 and 1992 when he and his family donated $100,525 to the Democrats.

Since Clinton embarked on his first Presidential campaign in 1991, the Riady family and Lippo Group's US subsidiaries have contributed more than $475,000 to the Democratic Party.

Aside from his position within the commerce department, John Huang was very active as a fund-raiser for the Democrats and specialised in raising money from Asian-American donors. It is estimated that during the 12 month period leading up to the 1996 presidential election, he was responsible for raising $5 million.

One of Huang's major coups was to solicit $427,000 from Arief Wiriadinata, a landscape architect, and his wife Soraya. They were immigrants in the US of Indonesian origin and lived in a working class neighbourhood in Virginia. In November 1995, the Wiriadinatas each made a $5,000 donation to the Democratic National Committee. In December 1995 they contributed a further $100,000. They returned to their homeland of Indonesia but continued to make donations until, by June, 1996, the total of their donations made was $427,000.

One side of the debate argues that the Wiriadinatas were simply expressing a strong desire to see Clinton elected and that despite their modest lifestyle and lack of apparent wealth, the Wiriadinatas, and Mrs Wiriadinata in particular, have 'private means'. This is no surprise as Mrs Wiriadinata is the daughter of the now deceased Hashim Ning, business partner of Mochtar Riady, one of the wealthiest men in Indonesia and John Huang's boss at Lippo. The more cynical observers believe that the Wiriadinatas were merely a conduit for illegal Lippo donations to the Democratic Party orchestrated by John Huang. The fact that Huang also brought in a $250,000 illegal donation from a South Korean company which had to be returned, only support the conspiracy theories.

Understandably, Newt Gingrich, the Republican Speaker of the House of Representatives, called for Congressional enquiries. "This is a potential abuse of the American system on behalf of an Indonesian billionaire in a way that we have never seen in American history." In reply, Al Gore, the Vice President, claimed: "There have been absolutely no violations of any law or regulations."

Regardless of who is right, fears have been raised in the US that the system is open to abuse and that attempts have been made to buy influence in Congress. What is at stake? Some say the Indonesians were buying acquiescence in their abuse of workers rights - abuses which had been criticised by Amnesty International. Others say favour was being curried via the Commerce Department to win 'most favoured nation' status, which under American law bestows valuable trading and commercial advantages on countries such as China.

Drawing Board

From the Washington Post, March 1997

There is a more worrying theory in Washington that the seeking of political funding by the Democrats has allowed penetration of the Clinton administration by Chinese intelligence, using the 'Trojan Horse' of the Lippo Group.

In November 1992 China Resources Bank, which is based in Hong Kong and is the official commercial arm of China's Ministry of Foreign Trade and Economic Co-operation, purchased a 15% share in the Hong Kong Chinese Bank owned by the Lippo Group. Western Intelligence sources believe the China Resources Bank is a front for Chinese Intelligence. In 1993 the China Resources Bank increased its shareholding in the Hong Kong Chinese Bank to 50% giving the Lippo Group a profit of $12 million.

Before moving to Arkansas in the mid 1980s, John Huang had worked for Lippo at the Hong Kong Chinese Bank. Following his appointment to the US Commerce Department, Huang had access to economic and trade intelligence provided by the CIA and Huang visited Peking on a trade mission with Ron Brown in July 1994, when there were $5.5 billion worth of trade deals to be signed. Between 1994 and 1996, Secret Service logs show Huang to have visited the White House in the region of 70 times and had several meetings with President Clinton. Mochtar Riady of Lippo himself made six trips to Washington during Clinton's first Presidential term and met the President several times on each visit. In September 1995 Riady and Huang met Clinton and pressed for the retention of China's most favoured trading nation status.

Further allegations being made in Washington are that for an investment in the Lippo Group China has obtained lucrative trade deals, access to the US president and influence upon US foreign policy.

As the allegations of sleaze fly around in Washington, there have been two unlikely converts to reform, and it is fitting to close this chapter by reference to them as each hails from the countries examined here: the USA and the UK. In November 1996, both Bob Dole, the Republican contender for the US Presidency, and Lord Beaverbrook, the former Conservative Party Treasurer, called for radical changes to be made in the rules. US Democrats have said Dole is an unlikely champion this cause having raised more than $100 million from donors throughout his political career. Equally, Lord Beaverbrook raised £38 million for the Tories between 1990 and 1992.

Dole has called for a ban on donations from companies, unions, wealthy individuals and foreigners. Lord Beaverbrook, speaking on a BBC television programme, said parties could be tainted by the prospect that donors influence policy : "For there to be a squeaky clean political arena, then you've got to remove the possibility of corruption." At present there are too many voters who believe in that possibility.

In **Britain,** investigators revealed the existence of a number of organisations and companies used to channel funds to the Conservative Party from corporate donors. The revelations, in 1989, drew attention to a series of companies, known as the River Companies, established in 1949 by the then Leader of the Opposition, Sir Winston Churchill. These companies, originally eight in number, were named after British rivers whose names began with the letters A to H. By 1989 five companies had been dissolved, leaving only those named after the rivers Arun, Bourne and Colne. It was alleged that between 1954 and 1963 the River companies received about £2.6 million from UK companies for onward transmission to the Conservative Party, this sum representing over a third of Conservative Party donations during the period. Organisations receiving funds from corporate donors for transmission to the Conservative Party included the pressure groups British United Industrialists and the Northern Industrial Protection Association.

The **Slovak** President, Michal Kovac, accused the Prime Minister Vladimir Meciar of wrongdoing in March 1993, alleging that Meciar had told him he wanted a political ally in control of privatisation programmes to obtain money for his political party.

The **South Korean** government agreed to a parliamentary investigation in April 1994 into allegations the country's main Buddhist group had been involved in making illegal contributions to President Kim Young-Sam's 1992 election campaign. The head of the order was reported to have resigned amid allegations he had demanded bribes from monks seeking appointments.

In October 1996 The Economist delivered a grim and, as events later proved, devastatingly accurate prediction as to what would happen in **Albania** when pyramid investment schemes collapsed. Albania's pyramid schemes - where new deposits are used to pay the interest on earlier investors moneys - drew the attention of the International Monetary Fund, which urged the government to put a stop to such dangerous financial practices. At that time, according to reports, 70% of Albanian families had money 'invested' in one pyramid scheme or another. The question was raised by The Economist article, as to whether the Albanian President Sali Berisha had the political will to tackle the problem given that the firm operating the largest pyramid scheme, Vefa, had made no secret of its contributions to the campaign funds of the President. In something of an understatement, The Economist stated: "When the collapse comes, depositors may not take it quietly." They did not, and complete anarchy followed quickly.

In the **USA,** investigators claimed in March 1997 that a former senior aide to President Clinton was paid more than $400,000 for campaign purposes by a dozen companies, including supporters of a $2 billion American Chinese property development in the Fujian province of China, a development endorsed by the Clinton administration. Details emerged during a blizzard of allegations of fund-raising techniques involving coffee mornings and overnight stays at the White House. Questions were raised as to whether these opportunities for meeting the President were the means to solicit campaign contributions. Clinton maintained there was no link between donations and the guests who visited the White House, but Republican congressmen demanded the appointment of an independent counsel to investigate their claims that the president sold access to the White House.

Chapter Five

OUTSIDE
INTERESTS

"Sometimes, the Devil is a gentleman,"
Percy Shelley

In the summer of 1996 British MPs displayed their legendary thickness of skin - the envy of many a rhinoceros - and voted in favour of awarding themselves a pay rise of 26%, which would have resulted in their basic salaries increasing to £43,000. The vote was taken at the end of a parliamentary period during which the reputation of politicians sank to previously unplumbed depths. There was a deluge of allegations of members using their public office for private enrichment through the acceptance of paid work outside parliament. The exposure of the scale of allowances payable to MPs cast a light on the hidden hypocrisy which currently pervades British politics.

In the world outside Westminster's ivory towers, pay rises of 3% are seen as more realistic. What made the MPs' apparent greed even more offensive in the eyes of the British public was that the rise took place amid a political argument about the devastating effect that a minimum wage of £3.50 an hour would have on the British economy. An opinion poll found that 75% of people regarded the proposed salary of £43,000 as being too high.

Sir Terence Higgins, former Conservative MP and Treasury Minister, claimed MPs pay has actually fallen in real terms over the past 30 years. But this is not so. The 1965 salary of £3,250, adjusted for inflation, would have produced a figure of £33,000 in 1996, which was just below the salary of £34,085 paid before the proposed increase. Of course, the increase was not to be made across the board - success after all, breeds success - 26% was for the back-benchers (who comprise the bulk of the House of Commons), 49% for Cabinet Ministers and a proposed 70% rise for the

Prime Minister, equating to a salary of £143,000. In fairness, John Major, the former Prime Minister, argued against the scale of the rises, pushing for a 3% rise on the premise that MPs should set an example when millions of public sector workers were subject to wage restraint.

But Sir Terence Higgins argued Parliament faced a recruitment problem because of low pay. He felt the right people would not be attracted unless pay was improved. There is some truth in this argument - MPs have fallen behind the pay level of professionals and even the civil servants who advise them. What is largely ignored, however, are the additional perks and payments made available to MPs. Car allowance is based on mileage and size of engine. In addition, MPs get free rail, sea or air travel between home, constituency and Parliament. Wives and children of MPs get free travel fifteen times per year between constituency and London. MPs also receive free stationery, national telephone calls and postal services from Parliament. There is also a secretarial and research allowance, and MPs from nine London constituencies have a supplement added to their salary. MPs with constituencies outside London may claim additional expenses for overnight accommodation while on parliamentary business.

Salaries paid to MPs might not attract so much undesired attention if MPs devoted all their time to Parliament. Many represent the public interest for some of the time and their own for the rest. Analysis of data from the House of Commons Library conducted by Donald Shell, a politics expert at Bristol University, under commission for The Sunday Times newspaper, casts doubts on claims by some MPs that having interests outside Parliament produce 'better' MPs. On average, MPs attend only two thirds of all Commons votes. According to Shell, the busiest MPs in the Commons before the recent general election were Labour's Dennis Skinner (nicknamed the 'Beast of Bolsover', for his pugnacious Commons oratory) and Harry Barnes, and several Tories including Piers Merchant, Alan Duncan, Michael Fabricant and the former MP Harry Greenway.

Shell spoke less favourably of other MPs, drawing particular attention to former ministers, though Shell's study concentrated only upon activity in the Commons and not in constituencies. He found that David Mellor, MP for Putney and former Heritage Secretary, contributed to four debates and asked only three parliamentary questions during the 1995-96 Parliament. Since he resigned his cabinet post in 1993, Mellor has taken on a number of interests outside the Commons and is a consultant to a number of companies with Middle Eastern connections. He subsequently lost his seat. Kenneth Baker, the former Conservative Party Chairman, made contributions to just four debates and asked two questions. In the Commons Register of Members Interests, he is shown as sitting on six boards, including Hanson PLC, two cable firms, an international telecommunications company and a firm of investment bankers.

Another senior Tory, Norman Lamont, MP for Kingston-upon-Thames and former Chancellor of the Exchequer, made contributions to two debates and asked three questions. Lamont holds directorships in First Philippine Investment Trust, Taiwan Investment Trust and the Indonesian Fund, among others.

Richard Needham, a trade and industry minister until the summer of 1995, contributed to two debates, and did not table a single oral or written parliamentary question. Soon after leaving his post as trade minister, Needham became a paid, non-executive director of GEC, a company with which he had had dealings while in his government post.

The adverse reaction to Needham's appointment to GEC was mirrored by the reaction to the appointment of Tim Eggar, the former Energy Minister, as part time chairman of an engineering company in late 1996. The engineering company had strong links to the energy industry. Eggar's salary was not disclosed, but was expected to be substantial. His brief was to provide strategic guidelines for all energy and process related matters and his part-time position (more than half the working week) was only a precursor to him taking up a full-time post after leaving the Commons after the 1997 election.

A week after Eggar signed on the dotted line, Steven Norris, the former London Transport Minister, was reported to be considering joining the Capitol City Bus company. Norris left the government in July 1996 and the Commons after the May 1997 election, but while in office he oversaw the privatisation of London bus companies. Although Capitol City was not one of the publicly-owned bus subsidiaries sold off by the Government, the company operated routes contracted out by London Transport.

"The shamelessness of this move - coming on top of Tim Eggar's move sideways from energy minister to oil company boardroom - will heighten the public impression that Tory Ministers legislate for their own futures rather than the national interest," said Brian Wilson from the Labour Party. Needham, Eggar and Norris had all acted perfectly legally.

The acid test must be the answer to the question: does the appointment of MPs and former ministers pay dividends for the employing companies? For this we must delve briefly into Whitehall privatisations and contract programmes which have recently covered parts of the Property Services Agency, Her Majesty's Stationery Office, Ministry of Defence homes, benefit offices, the Recruitment and Assessment service and the Treasury Building in Whitehall.

The £1.6 billion sale of Ministry of Defence residential property was made to Annington Homes, a consortium which includes Hambros Bank and AMEC. Hambros Bank is chaired by the senior Tory, Lord Hambro.

HMSO was bought by the Electra Fleming consortium for £54 million after an original offer from the same consortium of £175 million. The consortium includes the Electra Investment Trust, which has Tom King, the former Tory defence secretary on the board and the merchant bank, Robert Fleming, which employs Sir Tim Renton, former Tory chief whip, as a consultant. Robert Fleming has donated £675,000 to Tory Party funds. Cynics may perceive a pattern emerging.

The Property Services Agency sell-off involved a number of divisions including Building Management (Manchester) where W S Atkins, the engineering and design conglomerate, was paid £11.5 million to take the business over and given a five year guarantee of orders from the MoD. Building Management (South East and South West) was sold to AMEC and Pell Frischmann for £11.4 million. AMEC, which sold the business for £684 million, employs Sir Alec Cockshaw, chairman of the Overseas Project Board at the Department of Trade and Industry.

To secure help in matters of Government policy in areas such as the Private Finance Initiative and the lobbying of ministers, W S Atkins retained Sir Archibald Hamilton, MP for Epsom and Ewell, as a consultant at a cost of £6,500 per annum. Hamilton first entered the Commons in 1978 and was a parliamentary private secretary to Lady Thatcher, a Government whip and between 1988 and 1993, a defence minister.

In addition to his work for W S Atkins, Archie Hamilton in October 1996 had a world-wide profile of interests, including £1,000 per year from Woodgate Farms Dairy in Sussex, and a further £2,000 per year from Saladin Holdings, a company run by a former Special Air Services major, David Walker. The Government's Private Finance Initiative,, highlighted in Hamilton's work for W S Atkins, attracted a £12,000 per year consultancy with Merrill Lynch Europe Ltd., international investment bankers, who have expressed an interest in financing deals involving the sale of the social security office property and the leasing of the Treasury building. Sir Archie also performed consultancy work worth £45,000 for Litton Industries Inc., a US defence manufacturer, and held directorships in Leafield Engineering Ltd, a company involved in electronic, mechanical and explosive engineering, Siam Selective Growth Trust, Philippines Securities and First Philippine Investment Trust.

Hamilton has attracted criticism during his career. After he had resigned from the Ministry of Defence he ran into controversy when a company he formed - now dormant - made a bid for an Army training area which had been closed while he was a minister. Hamilton's connections with Saladin Holdings caused embarrassment when it was discovered that Saladin was trying to take over security arrangements for the Foreign Office.

Despite these incidents, Archie Hamilton has not broken any rules and his interests, all properly declared, illustrate how money may be properly earned by an ex-Cabinet minister. "It must be a good thing to get professional middle class people into this House," said Hamilton. "If they have got to do this on a salary of £32,000 a year [MPs' salary at the time], to be quite honest they are not going to come."

Hamilton was defending the rights of MPs to add to their parliamentary salary to attract the right candidates for public office. In speaking out, Hamilton was opposing reforms proposed by Lord Nolan, whose Committee on Standards in Public Life had been appointed in October 1994. Hamilton was expressing the view that MPs should not have to disclose their earnings from consultancies. Lord Nolan's committee was established in part due to sleaze allegations levelled at a number of Tory MPs. Here we must pause to recall an investigation by The Sunday Times. Sir Archie Hamilton returns to the tale later.

IN THE summer of 1994, with rumours abounding that some MPs were willing to ask Parliamentary questions for a fee, Jonathan Calvert, a young journalist from the four-strong Sunday Times investigative 'Insight' team, posed as a respectable businessmen and contacted 10 Tory MPs and 10 Labour MPs with a simple question: would they be prepared to ask a Parliamentary question in return for a fee of £1,000?

Four Conservative MPs were willing: Bill Walker asked for the money to be sent to charity; Sir John Gorst said he would ask the question without being paid a fee, suggesting he might be happy to discuss future arrangements. David Tredinnick and Graham Riddick agreed to accept 'cash for questions'. Riddick entertained Calvert to tea on the terrace of the House of Commons. He was told by the 'businessman' that he was considering buying a company called Githins Business Resources and wanted to know what government contracts it had.

Riddick confirmed he could acquire the information. Two days later, Tredinnick entertained the same reporter at the same venue - Calvert later admitted he had been terrified Riddick would spot him on the terrace with the MPs colleague. On this occasion, the reporter asked how many times a drug called Sithgin had been prescribed on the National Health Service, as he planned to invest in the company. Tredinnick agreed to seek out the information.

When the newspaper revealed the story, both MPs were suspended from their positions as Parliamentary Private Secretaries. The Sunday Times attracted a fair amount of criticism from Tory MPs for their 'entrapment' methods, but the paper defended itself, replying: "Far from allaying the fears that MPs are not disinterested representatives of the electorate, they merely succeeded in reinforcing the suspicion that many are interested mainly in lining their own pockets."

On 20th July 1994 the names of those members who would hear the case against Tredinnick and Riddick were made public. There was vociferous criticism as among those who would consider the affair were a number of Conservative MPs who held outside consultancies and directorships. On 19th October, following the return after the summer recess, it was announced that all hearings relating to the affair would be held in secret, whereupon the Labour and Liberal Democrat members withdrew from the committee.

On 20th October 1994, the Guardian newspaper added to the controversy by alleging that two junior ministers, Neil Hamilton at the Department of Trade and Industry and Tim Smith at the Northern Ireland Office, had accepted cash for asking questions in the House while both had been backbenchers. The Guardian claimed that Ian Greer Associates, a lobbying company, channelled payments to the two MPs at the rate of £2,000 per question, on behalf of businessman Mohamed Al-Fayed. In a conversation with Al Fayed, Greer allegedly said: "You have to rent MPs like London taxis at £2,000 a time for questions".

In generating business, it later became clear that Greer was prepared to make payments to MPs who introduced clients. One such recipient was the former Tory MP Sir Michael Griffiths, who belatedly declared the payment some years after it had been paid. It was Griffiths who introduced Greer to Neil Hamilton.

In 1985 Greer was approached by Mohamed Al Fayed, who was then involved in a battle with Lonrho for control of Harrods. Al Fayed was seeking to counter attacks upon himself and his

How the Guardian splashed the Hamilton story

brother, which were being mounted in the House of Commons by a number of Tory MPs. Greer put forward Neil Hamilton as Al Fayed's champion and thus set in train the events that would lead to what became known as the 'cash for questions' affair.

Hamilton, who first denied receiving money from Al Fayed, contrary to Al Fayed's version of events, asked a series of parliamentary questions and signed a number of early day motions which were beneficial to Al Fayed and Harrods. A memo from Greer to Al Fayed in March 1989 suggested that these questions were orchestrated: "Today agreed with Neil Hamilton, four questions (faxed to you earlier today)".

As more details of allegations against MPs accused of taking cash for asking parliamentary questions and lobbying emerged, the activities of MPs were investigated by the Commissioner for Standards, Sir Gordon Downey. It was alleged that Hamilton took payments from Ian Greer totalling £10,000, which were declared neither to ministers lobbied by him or to the Inland Revenue. It was also alleged he took thousands of pounds in envelopes from Al Fayed while promoting the latter's interests; a lengthy enquiry began under the command of Sir Gordon Downey.

FACED with uproar over allegations of sleaze within his government, John Major, the former Prime Minister, also established a committee on Standards in Public Life, to be chaired by Lord Nolan.

Ian Greer and Neil Hamilton issued writs against the Guardian for libel, but even this course of action required parliamentary manoeuvring which attracted criticism. In July 1995, Mr Justice May, in the High Court, halted the proposed libel action citing the 1689 Bill of Rights. It was held that this legislation, enacted to ensure the supremacy of Parliament, was overly prejudicial towards the Guardian newspaper's defence, due to the doctrine of parliamentary privilege. Hamilton's response was to argue that rules established three centuries before effectively prevented him from giving evidence on statements made in the House of Commons and thereby clearing his name.

Hamilton promoted his cause within Parliament and an amendment to the Defamation Act was passed allowing MPs to waive privilege. The change took effect in September 1996 and attracted criticism from many quarters, including politicians - from all parties - who feared it would appear that MPs could pick and choose when to claim immunity and parliamentary privilege to their own advantage.

But the case progressed. The Guardian prepared to defend the libel action, which centred on payments made for questions asked in the Commons, and an additional allegation made by The Guardian that Hamilton incurred a £4,000 bill during a free holiday at the Ritz Hotel in Paris, provided by Mr Fayed. As part of its defence, The Guardian subpoenaed John Major, Michael Heseltine (then the Deputy Prime Minister) and Richard Ryder (another senior Tory), to give evidence at the High Court.

Relevant official documents were requested in addition to the normal disclosures made by both sides in any libel action. Treasury solicitors delivered these official documents on Thursday, 26th September 1996, with a trial date of 1st October 1996 looming. However the day before the trial was due to commence, the action was dramatically abandoned by Hamilton and Greer, with both agreeing to pay some of the newspapers legal costs. Hamilton said that he was 'devastated' at having to withdraw, proclaimed his innocence again but said he lacked the money.

According to Hamilton a conflict of interest had arisen with Greer which would have entailed the postponement of the trial and the instruction of new lawyers at considerable cost. The Guardian took the understandable view that the evidence its legal team had assembled would have won the case and that Hamilton had withdrawn in disarray. Evidence assembled by the newspaper included statements from three Al-Fayed employees who alleged they had handed envelopes stuffed with cash to Hamilton and Greer.

The press had a field day; and yet more disclosures and allegations followed. During the evening of 1st October 1996, Hamilton admitted he had taken money from Greer on two occasions, for 'introductions', though he still denied taking money from Al-Fayed. Of the two payments, one was for £6,000, the other £4,000. "The commissions placed me under no obligation whatever, either to Ian Greer or his company," said Hamilton. "They were wholly unconnected to my position as an MP and similar payments are frequently made throughout industry to people in all walks of life."

It was also revealed that 24 MPs: 21 Conservative, two Labour and one Liberal Democrat had received donations from Ian Greer towards their election campaigns during the 1987 general election. This information came to light as a result of the examination of a confidential Conservative Central Office memorandum, voluntarily passed to lawyers acting for the Guardian during the libel case. Payments varied between £200 and £5,000 and were legal if they did not exceed spending limits in each constituency. They did not need to be declared to Parliament and there was no suggestion any of the recipient candidates had acted illegally. Greer had originally received the money from the Fayeds (£18,000) and Dave Allen of DHL, the postal courier group, (£11,000). Some of the recipients were from the top echelons of the Tory party.

While neither the candidate nor Conservative Central Office had acted illegally or improperly in this matter (the donations passing directly to the fighting funds of individual MPs for their local campaigns), the potential for embarrassment for the Conservative Party was highlighted in the Central Office memorandum.

The Labour and Liberal Democrat parties also had difficulties to deal with because similar payments had been made to the 1987 election campaign funds of Doug Hoyle, the former Labour MP, and Alan Beith MP (Deputy Leader of the Liberal Democrats). Again, though there is no suggestion these payments were illegal, or improper, the potential for embarrassment was clearly huge.

The affair claimed a labour casualty on 3rd October 1996, when

Baroness Turner of Camden, a Labour spokeswoman on Employment in the Lords, stepped down following her defence of Ian Greer on Channel Four television. Baroness Turner was a director of Ian Greer Associates, a position which she had properly declared in the register of members interests. Lady Turner had been a friend of Greer's for over 20 years and a member of his board for five years.

A further cause for concern arising from the Hamilton/Greer libel suit against The Guardian was the allegation, prompted by a disclosed memorandum, that David Willetts, a government minister, had tried to influence an independent Commons investigation into the cash-for-questions affair. The Guardian newspaper published its allegations against Hamilton on 20th October 1994. The same day Willetts had met Sir Geoffrey Johnson Smith, the chairman of the Select Committee on Members Interests. At the time Willetts was a junior whip, though by October 1996 he held the post of Paymaster General, and was considered a high flyer nicknamed 'Two Brains'.

The Select Committee on Members Interests was investigating Neil Hamilton's stay at the Ritz in Paris. The disclosed memorandum written by Willetts following his meeting with Geoffrey Johnson Smith contained this extract, "… said No 10 had got in a muddle about Committee on Members Interests. They claimed it had cleared Neil Hamilton, but actually this was only on a complaint about remarks of his, not on the new allegation. He is now expecting to receive a formal complaint about Hamilton receiving money etc. He could, (i) argue now sub judice and get Committee to set it aside, or, (ii) investigate it as quickly as possible, exploiting good Tory majority at present. We were inclined to go for (i), but he wants our advice."

If the contents of the memorandum bear the most obvious interpretation, then two methods of minimising action by the Members Interests Committee against Hamilton were considered. If this were true, Willetts should not have been trying to influence a committee intended to protect the reputation of the House. Sir Geoffrey should have neither discussed the affair with Willetts nor exhibited partisan loyalties by referring the matter to the Whips Office. Though this memorandum was written on 20th October 1994 its existence was not made widely known until October 1996.

The later stage of the Hamilton affair and the Willetts memorandum were addressed by the new regulatory process which had been suggested by Lord Nolan's Committee. On 14th October 1996, after three and a half hours of deliberation, the Standards and Privileges Committee asked Sir Gordon Downey, the Parliamentary Commissioner for Standards, to investigate the Neil Hamilton 'cash for questions' affair. Two days later, MPs agreed without a vote to refer the Willetts memorandum to the Standards and Privileges Committee.

There had been pressure from both the Labour Party and Liberal Democrats for John Major, the Prime Minister, to set up a judicial enquiry into the 'cash for questions' affair. The two leaders insisted they had no confidence in Sir Gordon Downey's enquiry as he lacked the powers to summon witnesses or

Sir Gordon Downey

evidence. Instead they called for a body to be set up under the Tribunals of Inquiry (Evidence) Act 1921, a mechanism which had traditionally been used to investigate serious allegations of corruption or misconduct in public life.

The Government response to this was two fold; firstly that the streamlined disciplinary machinery as recommended by Lord Nolan should be given the opportunity to perform; secondly, that a judicial enquiry would require changes to the 1689 Bill of Rights, which forbids the proceedings of Parliament to be 'impeached or questioned' other than in Parliament itself.

What then were the reforms suggested by Lord Nolan? Nolan recommended a tougher regime to regulate MPs, including the appointment of a Parliamentary Commissioner for Standards. The Commissioner has no powers to call for people or documents, but can initiate enquiries after receiving complaints from MPs or members of the public. The Commissioner also oversees the register of members interests, draws up the rules for MPs declaring interests and provides confidential advice to MPs on details of their declarations. One of Downey's first actions was the preparation of the new register, which involved, for the first time, MPs having to declare income from consultancies and directorships directly related to parliamentary activities.

This in itself led to criticism and ambiguity as to what constituted earnings from parliamentary services. Some MPs revealed earnings from consultancies and provided copy contracts for public inspection. Other MPs only declared some of their income. Sir Malcolm Thornton, at the time an MP, urged colleagues to observe the 'spirit of the rules' to avoid allegations. Sir Gordon Downey's view was: "I have made it clear that it is a matter for decision by MPs what they include in the register. But if MPs decide they are not providing parliamentary services, they have to take the consequences if ever there is a complaint that they have been doing so."

In addition to the appointment of a Parliamentary Commissioner, a new Standards and Privileges Committee was established to replace the earlier Members Interests Committee and the Privileges Committee. The new committee consists of 11 members and is chaired by the Leader of the House of Commons. It can be attended by the Attorney General and the Solicitor General, both of whom may speak but not vote. While the Hamilton 'cash for questions' affair was referred to Sir Gordon Downey, the Parliamentary Commissioner for Standards for investigation, the Willetts affair did not fall within the Commissioner's remit. Lord Nolan's report expressed the clear view that privilege issues such as those raised by the Willetts affair should be dealt with by the Standards and Privileges Committee.

The David Willetts affair came to a swift conclusion with televised hearings of the Standards and Privileges Committee on 11th November 1996, ending 200 years of secrecy during which even discussion in public of the committee's private deliberations could place an MP in contempt of the Commons. The committee agreed to open its doors to enable proceedings to be viewed after the Speaker of the House, Betty Boothroyd, demanded openness in the investigation of allegations.

David Willetts was examined upon his role in the affair and found himself subject to a number of searching questions and accusations from an MP of his own party: Quentin Davies. Davies told Willetts during the hearing there was a '180 degrees' gap between his report of a conversation with Sir Geoffrey Johnson Smith and his interpretation of it in a memorandum considered by the investigating Standards and Privileges Committee.

In his defence, Willetts stated his memorandum was a short manuscript note, not intended for later analysis and that the word 'wants' as in 'wants our advice' was intended to represent 'needs'. He denied Sir Geoffrey wanted advice from the whips and further denied seeking to influence the committee. He did, however, admit to imposing an 'artificial structure' on the conversation, using words in the note which were his own and not those of Sir Geoffrey. In addition, Willetts apologised for causing any confusion or misconception, blaming his inexperience as a whip for leading to the situation where he was seen as trying to influence the committee.

For his part, Sir Geoffrey Johnson Smith claimed under examination by the committee, that he had not needed the advice of Willetts. He believed that Willetts had misunderstood their 'chat' and that he had not sought such guidance, adding that if he had, he 'would not have used a junior whip as a conduit, preferring instead the Chief Whip, Alastair Goodlad.

On 11th December, 1996, the Standards and Privileges Committee released its concise report which was followed by David Willetts resignation as Paymaster General minutes later. Willetts, was accused of 'dissembling' in his account to the committee, a response which 'substantially aggravated the original offence'. The report went on to say that "in any future investigation of matters of privilege or of complaints about the conduct of members, it will be our normal practice to take evidence on oath." This recommendation marked a great change in that, henceforth, MPs would no longer be regarded as automatically 'honourable'.

The Willetts affair was held to be a crucial test for the new regulatory mechanisms adopted by Parliament following Lord Nolan's recommendations, and the result was seen as a victory with two contributory factors. Firstly, Willetts resigned immediately, even though no penalty was recommended and secondly, the hearings were televised, widely reported by the media and transparent.

One fear harboured by many was that party politics would cause friction within the committee and lead to its emasculation due to warring factions. One nominated member of the Standards and Privileges Committee was Sir Geoffrey Johnson Smith who, because of his involvement in the Willetts affair, stood down. At first glance it appeared his nominated successor to the committee would be a cause of inter-party strife. Sir Geoffrey's successor was Sir Archie Hamilton referred to earlier.

Sir Archie had been outspoken in favour of Neil Hamilton when the latter had been attacked by the media over the 'cash for questions' affair. Further, as detailed earlier, Sir Archie had many outside interests. At the end of the day, the fact that Sir Archie's interests were all permissible and properly declared, coupled with a belief that his defence of his namesake

71

was more to do with attacking 'trial by media', led to Sir Archie's appointment without objection.

Ernie Ross, a Labour MP, replaced Doug Hoyle MP on the same committee, after Hoyle had been linked to a donation from Ian Greer Associates. It was a tangled web.

The fact that the findings of the committee in the Willetts affair were unanimous was seen as a positive step in favour of self regulation, buoyed by Willetts resignation providing a clean and clear cut conclusion. But the worst was still to come for the Tories. The final Downey report, released two months after the May general election, was damning proof of sleaze tainting the former governing Conservative party. It offers a brilliant overview of the whole squalid saga.

The Tories were accused of delaying publication of the report until after the election, and when it was finally released, possible reasons for delay became clear. Neil Hamilton, the former Tory government minister, was found guilty of taking up to £25,000 from Mohamed Al Fayed, the owner of Harrods. Hamilton, Tim Smith - the former Northern Ireland minister, Michael Brown - the former government whip, and former Tory MPs Sir Andrew Bowden and Sir Michael Grylls were all found guilty of not publicly declaring payments received from either Al Fayed or Ian Greer, the parliamentary lobbyist who organised Al Fayed's campaign against Tiny Rowland's attempts to regain control of Harrods. If the report had been released before the general election, the outcome would have been even more disastrous for the Tories, and would almost certainly have led to demands for the expulsion of Hamilton and Smith from the Commons.

Bowden misled officials, and also failed to register a £5,000 campaign donation despite the fact that he probably knew it came from Al Fayed. Grylls "deliberately misled" a House of Commons Select Committee over the number of commission payments he had received and also failed to declare important interests during his dealings with government ministers and public officials. Brown "persistently and deliberately" failed to declare crucial interests during his dealings with ministers and officials. The most serious condemnation, however, was reserved specifically for Hamilton and Smith. "The evidence that Mr Hamilton received cash payments directly from Mr Al Fayed in return for lobbying services is compelling; and I so conclude," said Sir Gordon Downey in a simple statement.

Tim Smith actually admitted to Sir Gordon Downey that he had received up to £25,000 in cash from Al Fayed for 'lobbying services'. But for the investigative journalists who spent months researching the activities of a small group of Tory MPs accused of sleazy double-lives, the most important lines in the report were those substantiating Hamilton's lying and cheating. The former MP for Tatton - trounced at the general election by Martin Bell, the former BBC war correspondent who stood against him on an anti-corruption ticket - was also accused by Sir Gordon of concealing cash payments and lavish hospitality from US Tobacco, another client of Ian Greer. There were the two separate stays at the exclusive Ritz hotel in Paris, owned by Al Fayed, and stays in other luxury Parisian apartments at Al Fayed's expense. Then there were the lies told to Michael Heseltine (the former Deputy Prime Minister) about payments from Greer, coupled with the misleading of other government ministers - such as David Mellor and Edwina Currie -when Hamilton was lobbying to introduce Skoal Bandits, the banned chewing tobacco, into Britain. Hamilton's behaviour "fell well below the standards expected of Members of Parliament".

MOHAMED AL FAYED'S evidence is a powerful argument for independent regulation of MPs activities: "I was familiar with the concept that professional men expected their fees," he said, "but I was taken aback and disappointed that no one at that time [during his battle for control of Harrods] would speak up for me in the Mother of Parliaments unless they were paid for their lobbying services. They should have declared those payments but did not, contrary to the Parliamentary rules."

So was Hamilton contrite and apologetic amid this onslaught? On the contrary, he immediately announced his intention to appeal and started demanding money from the media for answering their questions - his formidable wife Christine initially asked for £275 from a television crew, but later dropped her price to £75. Hamilton also said that - if he had enough money - he would consider re-launching a libel action against The Guardian newspaper. "I'm extremely disappointed and devastated," said Hamilton. "I am perplexed more than anything else. I totally deny any dishonesty. The only evidence against me is from his [Al Fayed's] paid employees. He (Downey) says the evidence I took this money is compelling, but he can't say when it was taken and how much was taken, why it was given or where it went."

Hamilton went on: "I was a minister in the government 1992-1994. I was

Sleaze, as viewed by a Guardian cartoonist

a DTI minister. Mr Fayed was suing the DTI at the time in the European Court of Human Rights. If I had wanted money from Fayed, I could have had it by the furniture-van-load if I had been prepared to reopen the DTI inquiry which condemned him as a liar and a fraud and if I had passed him information under the table." Then came an astonishing comment: "The reason he has released this barrage against me was that when I got into a position to help them, I did not want to know. So what this proves is not the government is corrupt but the opposite: the Government could not be corrupted."

Tim Smith behaved more honourably, apologising and saying: "I am very sorry that my conduct, as Sir Gordon Downey has described it, fell well below the standards expected of MPs. I can only say in my defence that it seemed less obvious at the time than it does with the benefit of hindsight what was the right course of action to take." There were immediate calls for both men to be expelled from the Conservative Party.

The response of the public and press was unequivocal. The Times ran a devastating comment article the day after publication of the report under the headline, "A damning judgement on the arrogance of power". The Times commented: "Had the Downey report on the 'cash for questions' scandal been published, as it should have been, before the general election, the Conservatives might have suffered an electoral catastrophe rather than a mere disaster. Now, two months later, the MPs condemned by Sir Gordon Downey are out of the Commons anyway. The fate of the governing party has already been decided. All that remains is the reputation of five former Members of Parliament. But, as a verdict on the integrity of two members of the last Government, Sir Gordon's report is devastating." The article was highly critical of Hamilton, and to a lesser extent Tim Smith. "William Hague [the new Tory leader] can show that he genuinely intends to make a 'fresh start' by disowning all the guilty men in the Downey report and ensuring that his party never lends its name to them again."

The Conservative Party's response? "The individuals concerned will wish to consider how they wish to respond to Sir Gordon Downey's serious findings. The Conservative Party wishes to see such matters fairly and rigorously dealt with," said William Hague, the party's new leader. An announcement from Tony Blair's office said: "We are taking action as a government on party funding and the corruption of MPs. We have emphasised repeatedly we will raise standards in political life."

For the Liberal Democrats, Charles Kennedy said the report was seminal and salutary: "The sad truth is that on the part of a number of MPs there has been disingenuous and dishonest behaviour. Phrases such as 'deliberately misled', 'persistently and deliberately' failing to declare interests, and 'positively misleading' speak for themselves."

Quentin Davies, the well-respected Conservative MP and member of the Commons Standards and Privileges Committee known for his robust independence, said the whole investigation had been a morass of allegations, claims and counter-claims. "After all of that, now you can be certain that the facts have been effectively established... the most important things in terms of public confidence in our institutions is that everyone should be confident that there is no danger of a cover-up."

Meanwhile the Guardian gave itself a well-deserved pat on the back: "...we called Neil Hamilton 'A Liar and a Cheat'," said Alan Rusbridger, the paper's editor. "That verdict is now official. Sir Gordon's report is a complete vindication of all the work by the Guardian over nearly four years. It is a detailed, thorough and damning demonstration of every single lie that Neil Hamilton has spread during that period."

THE ALLEGATIONS laid against the Tory MPs by The Guardian and other newspapers required a major enquiry, and the three-volume Downey report was a textbook example of a major parliamentary investigation. Sir Gordon, a former public-spending watchdog, and his team had a voracious, pedantic appetite for detail, even subjecting a number of disputed documents to ESDA (electrostatic deposition analysis) forensic tests to check their authenticity. Some have accused the Downey team of being too forensic in analysis, resulting in a lengthy two-year investigation when two months were what was required. But while many claim the cash-for-questions saga took far too long to be sorted out, it was an almost unique situation requiring a judicious and responsible approach: two years may have been what was needed.

New rules have since been introduced to counter sleaze in British politics, but what is needed now, in my view, is a further tightening of the codes of procedure, particularly on disclosures of payments. The current system, within which MPs are seen as 'honest chaps' to be treated differently from the public at large, is not adequate. While MPs are generally subject to the criminal law, it has, until recently, been widely accepted that in relation to matters such as bribery and corruption, only Parliament can perform the regulatory function.

This belief is based upon assertions by the Royal Commission on Standards of Conduct in Public Life in 1976, which held that Parliament was not a 'public body' as defined by the Public Bodies Corrupt Practices Act 1889 , or the wider definition provided by the Prevention of Corruption Act 1916, which covers 'public authorities of all descriptions'.

In addition, the common law offence of accepting a bribe in a public office may not be employed, as argued by the same Royal Commission, against MPs because they (in the opinion of the Commission) do not hold 'public office'.

This point has, to date, not been tested by the courts. It seems odd that in related matters, the courts have decided that an 'office' is a 'subsisting permanent, substantive position' which exists independently of the holder and is capable of being 'filled in succession by successive holders'. MPs would certainly appear to be office-holders and Lord Buckmaster in 1922 (in relation to a different issue) defined public office as 'an office, the payment of which is not provided out of a private fund'.

Those who resent intrusion into the disciplinary affairs of the House would also rely on the Bill of Rights of 1689 which states that what MPs say and do in Parliament cannot be questioned in any court of law. Critics would say, however, that if Neil Hamilton could easily secure an amendment to the law allowing him to waive privilege for his libel suit with the Guardian, then the doctrine of privilege is already weakened. If it is already weakened then it is capable of further modification to engender public confidence, which has been badly damaged due to the perception MPs may accept payment which, if they were civil servants or local councillors, would render them liable to prosecution.

In June 1997, the new Labour Home Secretary, Jack Straw, announced proposals to make MPs subject to new anti-corruption laws proposed for consideration by the Law Commission the intention of revising and simplifying the legislation already in place. Straw went the extra mile by announcing his intention to make MPs clearly liable under these proposals. This move is to be applauded.

An Australian judge commenting on a 1923 case of an MP receiving money from outside Parliament said, "it impairs his capacity to exercise a disinterested judgement ... from the point of view of the public interest, and makes him a servant of the person who pays him, instead of a representative of the people." I do not think the problem can be put more simply.

The People's Trust, a non-parliamentary body committed to promoting the reform of the UK political system reported that in 1996, 315 Conservative MPs held 287 well-paid directorships and 146 consultancies, while 29 Labour MPs shared 60 directorships and 43 consultancies. In full-page advertisements in national newspapers, the organisation lambasted MPs for allowing power, privilege and money to replace duty, honour and decency in the corridors of Westminster. While attacking the greed and self interest of some MPs the advertisements compared the refusal of a 3% pay rise for nurses to the 26% increase secured by MPs against a vote in Parliament. The vote to spend £6 million to improve the members tea-room at the House of Commons drew equally scathing comment.

Chapter Six

GATEKEEPERS

"There was a door to which I found no key. There was a veil past which I could not see." Edward Fitzgerald

W HEN faced with obstacles in life, the most successful are also the most resourceful, those who find workable solutions to problems. But how often is the phrase heard, "It's not what you know, it's who you know." and how many problems are solved through 'contacts'? Such contacts may be made on an informal basis, socially, professionally, or as part of a structured approach to influence outcomes. Where undue influence or favouritism is suspected, however, public concern is raised. Those among us who hold the means to provide access to business opportunities, or to power, are sometimes known as the 'gatekeepers'.

While American conspiracy theorists must give thanks every night at bedtime for the founding of the Central Intelligence Agency (CIA), their British-based brethren must rely upon a far older institution, that of freemasonry. These institutions share a common feature: a veil of secrecy covers their activities.

The CIA would see this as an operational requirement, but in the case of freemasonry, such secrecy attracts suspicion in a way that is not mirrored through membership of other organisations or clubs. This is in spite of all candidates offering themselves as potential Masons declaring that in doing so they are not "influenced by mercenary or other unworthy motives". Jerry White, the Local Government Ombudsman, has summed up the problem elegantly. "Rightly or wrongly," he said, "freemasonry is generally viewed with suspicion among non-Masons, not least because of the secrecy attached to 'The Craft'."

Since the office of Ombudsman was first established there have been more than 30 complaints of undue Masonic influence being brought to bear upon local and regional councils. All have been rejected, but the level of public concern expressed about Masonic influence has led to the publication of nine reports, even though such reports would not normally be produced following the dismissal of a complaint.

The problem lies in the public perception of the power of freemasonry rather than hard evidence of abuse of authority or corrupt practice by Masons. It is hardly surprising that those indulging in secret practices, bonded by secret oaths, should fall under suspicion.

The focus for concern is the widely held belief that Masons will favour others of a like persuasion, whether in business, employment or some would go so far as to say, justice. Many believe such favoured status opens many doors. The suspicion of easy access to reward is grounded in Masonic ritual which states that any freemason should, "relieve and befriend" Masons in need of help, suggesting, "the most kindly and the most palliating and the most favourite circumstances in extenuation of his conduct even when justly liable to reprehension and blame."

In the light of such ritual, it should have been obvious that the recent appointment by the government of a freemason, Sir Frederick Crawford, to head a new commission to investigate miscarriages of justice, would lead to protests. The Liberal Democrat MP Alan Beith, while never questioning Sir Frederick's integrity, drew attention again to the problem of perception and urged him to renounce his membership, "... given the number of police officers, especially Metropolitan Police, who are freemasons and the obligations which the movement puts on them towards each other, I'd rather see the new chairman distance himself."

The appointment of Crawford, with its attendant publicity for freemasonry in public life, was followed only weeks later when Chief Constables called upon officers and civilian police support staff to register their position within the ranks of freemasonry. The Association of Chief Police Officers (ACPO) also called upon the Home Office to introduce legislation requiring officers to register membership of any organisation demanding a bond of loyalty from its members and thereby creating a potential for conflicts of interest. Speaking about the proposals for a voluntary register of interest in the first instance, Paul Whitehouse, Chief Constable of Sussex said: "What we are trying to do is to reassure the public that everyone in the police service is determined to deliver a fair service." He also echoed the point made earlier: "It's the secrecy that's the cause for concern. After all, there's not a widespread feeling that being a Rotarian or a Lions Club member presents a threat."

The announcement made by ACPO in October 1996 came only days after the House of Commons Home Affairs Select Committee announced it was seeking evidence for its own enquiry into freemasonry in the police and the judiciary. The committee later took evidence from the public face of British freemasonry - the United Grand Lodge - as well as Chief Constables, the Police Federation and the Lord Chancellor.

The findings were published in March 1997 with recommendations that judges, magistrates and police officers belonging to Masonic Lodges should be required to declare such membership. The report stated: "nothing so much undermines public confidence in public institutions as the knowledge that some public servants are members of a secret society, one of whose aims is mutual self advancement." As a balance to this, acknowledgement was made of the fact that "a lot of honest people derive innocent social pleasure from membership".

There are, however, well documented instances of couplings between crime and Masons. In the 1960s the Scotland Yard Obscene Publications Squad contained twelve officers who were jailed for taking bribes from pornographers. All the officers, including the Squad's senior officer, Detective Chief Superintendent Bill Moody, were Masons.

Moody had even helped one of the pornographers to become a member of his Lodge. Under questioning from the Commons Home Affairs Committee, Commander Michael Higham, grand secretary of the United Grand Lodge of England revealed that 277 freemasons had been forced to leave the craft between 1987 and 1996 for criminal activities. "If they fall foul of criminal law, we almost invariably expel them," he said. Between 1946 and 1986, only twelve expulsions took place, a figure attributed by Commander Higham to the belief that earlier Masons did the 'honourable thing' and resigned.

These figures pale into insignificance when one considers the effect that the 'Propaganda Due' (P2) Lodge in Italy had upon that country after a scandal involving it broke in 1981. A contemporary Italian Government report described the Lodge as 'a secret sect that has combined business and politics with the intention of destroying the country's constitutional order'. Founded in 1966, the Lodge was intended to be a group of powerful men who would be useful to freemasonry. Three years later, headed by

Licio Gelli, referred to as Venerable Master, the Lodge was a magnet for many who believed Gelli and P2 could further their chosen careers.

Under the cover of P2, Gelli extracted valuable information from its members, a source of power which he used for his own ends. P2 membership files were seized and contained a list of almost 1,000 of Italy's most powerful men, including three Cabinet members, several former Prime Ministers, 43 MPs, 54 top civil servants, 30 generals, eight admirals, 19 judges, police chiefs, bankers and journalists. Gelli had constructed a state within a state with freemasons dispersed through every centre of power in Italian society.

I am not suggesting any such conspiracy exists in the United Kingdom. But such a nightmare scenario certainly puts into perspective the evidence given to the Home Affairs Select Committee on freemasonry in the police and judiciary by Martin Short, author of 'Inside the Brotherhood'. Short gave his evidence on the first day of the inquiry and alleged at least two Lodges exist in the Houses of Parliament with an unknown level of membership. Short also went on to say that in his opinion, freemasons who were public servants in any capacity should declare that interest and that such a list of interests should be made publicly available, a move presumably intended to allay public fears and suspicions of the exercise of undue influence or favouritism.

The preoccupation with Masonic influence in the United Kingdom is partially explained by its role in a massive corruption scandal - the Poulson affair. In their book 'Web of Corruption', the definitive story of the affair, the authors Raymond Fitzwalter and David Taylor state: "If the Church was one of the focal points in Poulson's life, the freemasons lodge was another. In business much of what he did was behind closed doors, and he was naturally attracted to the secret society of freemasonry, which practised morality, charity and obedience to the law and yet offered its members enormous political and business advantages."

John Poulson became Master of two Lodges and was elected Provincial Grand Deacon of Yorkshire, where he exploited freemasonry to the full. The opportunities available were highlighted in a submission made by the Society of Labour Lawyers to the Government's Royal Commission of Standards of Conduct in Public Life, which ran between 1974 and 1976. In the submission, reference was made to the desirability of declarations by local councillors of "all direct and indirect interests, financial and otherwise" at every council or committee meeting. In clarification, the submission went on: "We say 'financial or otherwise' because it is well within the experience of our members that secret decisions or understandings are reached in places which would not exist if generally known. In particular, we refer to 'town hall Lodges' which, we know, existed at each and every one of the local authorities concerned in recent criminal proceedings (Bradford, Birmingham, Newcastle and Wandsworth amongst others) and almost all the defendants were members. These Lodges take into membership leading councillors across the political divide together with a limited number of senior officers to the prejudice of the justification of the two party system - that of public dispute and decision - and to the prejudice of the proper relationship between councillor and officer. It is no part of our message to decry the traditions and charitable good work of the Masonic movement; we imagine that the national leaders would be as distressed as anyone if they knew of the extent to which the town hall Lodges were used, at the very least, to ease communication of matters which would never have been communicated at all in the full glare of publicity."

The point made in the submission about the concern of the national leaders of freemasonry at the abuse of the movement was echoed by the librarian and curator of the Grand Lodge Museum, John Hamill, when giving evidence to the Commons Home Affairs Committee in February 1997. This followed reference to the Poulson affair and its Masonic links by Chris Mullin, Labour MP for Sunderland South.

Hamill made the point that such people "were crooks who happened to be freemasons. They were not crooks because they were freemasons." But secrecy creates suspicion which is inflamed when actual criminal acts are discovered which can be linked to such secrecy. For the wrongs of the few, all are tarred with the same brush.

Never one to miss an opportunity to secure the inside track and an unfair commercial advantage, Poulson did not trust to Masonic contacts alone. Using his associate T. Dan Smith's public relations companies, Poulson passed money to numerous councillors to secure lucrative contracts and commissions within the gift of local government.

This leads to another area of public concern and public suspicion of the exercise of undue influence - public relations and commercial lobbyists. While freemasonry may be seen as an informal system of access to opportunities to be exploited by those so minded, commercial lobbying is formalised, accepted and seen by many as a necessary component of a democratic process which at times is in danger of "information overload".

Well reasoned, well researched and well presented arguments all aid the business of Parliament. Concern arises with the perception that some lobbyists are motivated for cash not conviction, sell favoured access to thwart the small man and cut ethical corners to influence policy. In itself, lobbying is desirable and necessary in an open system of government. However it is the methods used by some operators which arouse suspicions.

LOBBYING in Britain is an industry worth more than £500 million per year. One man at the cutting edge of the business is Sir Tim Bell, who heads a number of public relations companies gathered under the umbrella of the publicly listed firm Chime Communications. Chime is valued at £20 million; Bell is the largest private shareholder. He was also the Chairman of the advertising company Saatchi and Saatchi at the time when it secured the account for the Tory advertising campaign in the 1979 election. Thus a relationship began between Bell and Margaret Thatcher which lasted throughout the 1983 and 1987 general election campaigns.

Bell's Mayfair offices are a monument to his powerful friends and clients; the staircase is lined with photographs of Margaret Thatcher, Rupert Murdoch, F W de Klerk, the Sultan of Brunei and Lords Weinstock, Hanson and King. On his team, Bell has two men who have worked as senior political advisers to two Prime Ministers - Stephen Sherbourne to Margaret Thatcher and Jonathan Hill to John Major. Other employees have worked for the European Commission, as advisers to government, for political parties, or in Whitehall.

And what of the role of Bell's companies? "We act as a bridge, an advocate or a hired hand..." he said. "We will give advice to anybody who we think we can do a decent job for and who will reward us properly."

John Major's political secretary at one time was Howell Jones, a close friend of Bell. When asked how useful it was having contacts in 10 Downing Street, Bell replied, "It's extremely useful because they will probably take your call. Whether they will supply you with information is another matter. Half our business is knowing who to talk to."

Client confidentiality prevents Bell speaking about many of his companies operations. He has, however, spoken about the activities of G-Tech, the US parent company of Camelot, which operates the UK National Lottery franchise. Realising the value of the franchise, G-Tech hired Bell, other lobbying agencies, and a number of former Tory Cabinet Ministers, to advise on governmental procedures and decision-making. Bell commented: "They were buying everybody up so their opponents couldn't use them ... I can't see anything wrong with it."

With the election of a Labour government in the General Election of 1997, it remains to be seen what is the future for the lobbying industry. Some practitioners feel there will be a greater need for lobbyists to explain to industrialists the workings of the Labour Party.

Whatever happens in Britain, however, lobbying is going from strength to strength in the European Commission. With every expansion of EC influence and European Parliamentary power, the number of lobbyists increases. Before the emergence of plans for a single European market, there were estimated to be 300-500 lobby groups in Brussels. Following the mass of legislation associated with the 1992 implementation, there are now believed to be 10,000 lobbyists. Along the Avenue Louise in Brussels, law firms and public relations consultancies compete for office space to ply a lucrative trade.

Fears that the increased level of lobbying would lead to 'sleaze' and the buying of favours has led to new codes of conduct being drawn up. The guidelines, however, are seen as less exacting than those enforced in Washington, where the activities of lobbyists also give cause for concern. The broad aim of the European reforms is to make the whole lobbying process more transparent and thereby less open to abuse, the establishment of a directorate for openness, communication and information forming a central plank of this policy.

ATTENTION to the activities of lobbyists in the United Kingdom was of course focused during 1996 and the early months of 1997 upon the activities of Ian Greer, formerly of the lobbying firm Ian Greer Associates and a man who at the age of 24 was the youngest ever Conservative Party agent. Having built up a network of political friends, Greer established one of the United Kingdom's first political consultancies in 1969.

As previously discussed, Greer became embroiled in the cash for questions affair but the extent of his business activities shows just how profitable lobbying has become. His business grew to encompass such clients as British Airways, Cadbury-Schweppes, Coca Cola, Midland Bank and latterly and disastrously (for Greer) Mohamed Al Fayed, the owner of the Harrods department store. But Greer was not alone. By the 1980s, there were literally hundreds of competing consultancies operating in and around Whitehall.

It is ironic therefore to discover that the United States Congress has more powers over British registered political consultancies advising US companies, than the House of Commons does over such bodies operating in Britain. In the US, such consultancies is bound by the provisions of the Foreign and Corrupt Practices Act, which grants officers,

The Guardian, March 1997

acting on behalf of Congress, a right to inspect the records of the consultants. Sadly, this power is not available to the British Parliament.

In 1994 the Commons suggested a system of self-regulation and the Association of Professional Political Consultants (APPC) was established with Ian Greer as a founder member. There is a publicly available register deposited with the House of Commons which lists firms, consultants and clients. Additionally there is a code of conduct for all member firms and their employees, banning financial dealings with MPs.

The weakness, however, lies in the fact that the APPC can only regulate those firms which choose to join its ranks. At present, many are free to operate outside the professional rules. As Charles Miller, the association secretary put it, "Some lobbyists choose not to be regulated. We can exercise no sanction over them regardless of their activities. We have to ensure that everyone who claims to deal for gain with institutions of the

Government work to most scrupulous standards." In support of Miller's stance, Andrew Gifford, chairman of the APPC, wrote to the then Leader of the House, Tony Newton, urging the adoption of a formal system of regulation to be administered by the Commons.

Systems of regulation do not always achieve desired ends, however. Sometimes not enough thought is given to the wording of regulations to achieve the desired end. Under Parliamentary rules drawn up in the wake of the Nolan enquiry and governing outside interests, MPs are required to disclose earnings and contracts if the consultancy involves 'the provision of services in his or her capacity as an MP'. However no such details are required if they maintain the consultancy has nothing to do with parliamentary work. This is a strange anomaly.

As Roger Willoughby, acting registrar of Member's interests at the Commons said in January 1997, he had to accept the word of MPs their outside work was unrelated to their Parliamentary role. "Fortunately for us, the Commons resolution never said 'arising out of your membership of Parliament' - which would have been a very different proposition," he added.

Such provisions allowed the former national heritage secretary and foreign office minister David Mellor MP for Putney, until he lost his seat in the May 1997 General Election, to avoid disclosing details of his earnings from a number of consultancies in the Register of Members Interests by claiming his consultancies were 'not dependent in any way upon my being an MP'. By April 1997 Mellor's business interests included consultancies for 11 companies, which sources estimated had earned him in excess of £1 million in four years.

He has purchased a £1.25 million house near Tower Bridge, London, a £360,000 house in South West London for his former wife, and he operates from a plush office in Mayfair. Much of Mellor's activity as a consultant relates to the Middle East, an area where he attracted attention in 1990, when as a junior foreign office minister during a visit to the West Bank and Gaza, he rounded upon an Israeli Colonel over the treatment of Palestinians. Further pro-Arab comments followed, during a visit to Abu Dhabi when he said, "In my whole political career, I haven't felt I've said anything more right than what I said in the occupied territories."

Much of Mellor's business comes from consultancy work for British arms companies selling weapons to the Middle East. One of Mellor's contracts is with GKN, the arms and engineering company which is providing Piranha armoured vehicles to Qatar. Other Mellor clients include Vosper Thorneycroft, Shorts and British Aerospace, all selling weaponry to the same country. In The Sunday Times of 26th January 1997, Nicholas de Jongh, GKN's director of public affairs, was quoted in relation to David Mellor's efforts for his company. When asked if GKN's contract had anything to do with Mellor's role as a politician, the newspaper reported Mr de Jongh's reply as being: "I think it must do. He hasn't got much else to offer has he? We are not the sort of organisation that has ornamental advisers around. We cover these things with commercial confidentiality and we never discuss who we employ and on what terms."

And what does David Mellor actually do for his money? In an earlier article The Sunday Times quoted an intermediary active in the Middle East describing Mellor as a "highly paid door opener".

WITH ITS VORACIOUS appetite for high technology equipment and armaments, the Middle East is a rich source of income for gatekeepers. During the 1970s and early 1980s the role of supreme gatekeeper was played by the flamboyant Adnan Khashoggi, a man who straddled the Western and Arab worlds and made huge fortunes through meeting the needs of the West to sell and the Arab world to buy. Khashoggi courted heads of state and deal makers throughout the globe. While he remains a powerful figure to this day, Khashoggi saw a decline in his influence with his involvement in the 'Irangate' affair and his arrest and subsequent acquittal in 1988 on charges of concealing moneys belonging to ex-President Marcos of the Philippines. Even Richard Nixon was courted by Khashoggi.

'Tricky Dicky' is the hero of another 'trade bridge' or gatekeeper between the Arab and Western worlds: Jonathan Aitken the former MP and author of a 600 page biography of the disgraced US President. In June 1997, following the collapse of a libel action brought by Aitken against The Guardian newspaper and Granada television, UK newspapers detailed the former defence procurement ministers' contacts with the Arab world which brought him wealth and ultimately led to his downfall. Aitken had been managing director of the investment company Slater Walker (Middle East) Ltd and later joined the board of Al Bilad (UK), the Saudi royal family's investment vehicle in the UK in Britain. Other business ventures followed, most relying upon Middle Eastern connections, the most important being Saudi Prince Mohammed bin Fahd. Aitken's business acumen helped him to amass a fortune reputedly worth millions, but he is one of the most prominent victims of the renewed British debate on standards in public life. His story is a cautionary tale for any politician contemplating a cover-up and a reminder of the power of investigative journalists.

At the time of writing, Aitken, once dubbed the tallest and handsomest man in British politics, is waiting to hear whether he will be prosecuted for perjury and conspiracy to pervert the course of justice after the dramatic collapse of his libel trial against the Guardian newspaper. In the space of a few days Aitken lost his marriage, his career and a sizeable chunk of his fortune in a bonfire of vanities at the High Court in London. It is an igno-minious situation for a man described by some commentators as a future Prime Minister, and yet it all began with a simple little lie.

In September 1993, Aitken, then the minister for defence procurement at the Ministry of Defence, had been staying in the luxurious Ritz hotel in Paris at the same time as a number of Arab friends. One of the other hotel guests was Said Ayas, the personal assistant to Prince Mohammed bin Fahd, a son of the Saudi king. Aitken had advanced his career by building good relationships with the House of Saud and at the time of his Ritz visit one of Aitken's jobs was to ensure the desert regime continued to buy from British arms manufacturers many of the unnecessary military arms, ships and planes which litter Saudi Arabia. During his stay at the Ritz, Aitken talked with the Prince about a possible deal in which Britain would sell four submarines to the Saudis.

His visit to the spectacular hotel may have passed off without note or memory if the owner of the hotel had not noticed him talking with the Saudis. Mohamed Al Fayed, owner of Harrods and the Paris Ritz hotel, was in the Ritz by chance and saw Aitken with the Saudi arms dealers. "It was like the Attorney General sitting with Al Capone," Al Fayed is reported to have said.

Al Fayed features elsewhere in this book. The Egyptian-born multi-millionaire courted several Conservative MPs before he grew disillusioned with the government when they refused to grant him British citizenship, and started leaking details dubious activities. All were catalogued to be revealed to the press in the last years of John Major's government - many believe that in helping to perpetuate and then expose the aura of sleaze around the Conservatives he was the single most important figure in ensuring the Tories were thrashed during the 1997 elections.

So Al Fayed was aware of the importance of the meeting between the Saudis and Aitken. He made some enquiries. Who had paid Aitken's bill, he asked his compliant staff at the front desk? The answer delighted Al Fayed: it was Ayas who had paid for a minister of the British crown to receive hospitality at one of the world's most expensive hotels. Al Fayed is a sharp man, and he knew Aitken had accepted a 'gift' (in having his stay paid for him) which is banned under Cabinet Office guidelines because of the obvious conflict of interest. Al Fayed knew it could be used against the Tories.

Shortly afterwards, the Guardian newspaper was contacted by Al Fayed's office and told of the story. The journalists were interested, but not overly excited. "We knew he [Aitken] could just bluff his way out of it," said one. "All he had to say was that he had bought Ayas and his group an expensive meal, and Ayas had paid for the room as a quid pro quo." But he didn't.

The Guardian wrote to Aitken at the Ministry of Defence asking him to account for the meeting and its relevance to his job as a government minister. The same day, journalists from the paper contacted Ayas with similar questions. Ayas was open; the minister was not. He tried to mislead the reporters, which aroused their suspicions that Aitken had something to hide. "We knew instantly there was something fishy," said a reporter involved in the case.

IT HAD BEEN a quiet Sunday afternoon at the cashiers desk at the Ritz when a dark-haired woman with Latin features and a French accent had stepped forward to pay the bill for Monsieur Aitken in room 526. Until his case collapsed in the High Court, Aitken had spent three years telling reporters, the Prime Minister, lawyers and then a judge that the woman was his wife Lolicia, who happens to be blonde.

The woman who actually paid the minister's bill on behalf of Ayas was Manon Vidal, a glamorous 38-year-old former model who worked as a personal assistant to Saudi princes, travelling in their entourage with bags stuffed with money and cheques. Vidal happens to have the dark hair remembered so accurately by those working behind the desk.

Yet still Aitken lied. He could not admit to having been a guest of the

Arabs, for although it may not have been a case of outright corruption, such hospitality would have had more than a whiff of sleaze about it. Aitken claimed his wife had travelled from Switzerland to pay the bill, and had used cash because her terrible dyslexia made it difficult for her to use credit cards.

Aitken's case is a textbook study of the slow fall of a man pursued. He could not lose face, and decided to make an example of the Guardian. "If it has fallen to my destiny to start a fight to cut out the cancer of bent and twisted journalism in our country with the simple sword of truth and the trusty shield of British fair play, so be it. I am ready for the fight," said Aitken pompously as he announced his intention to sue in April 1995.

But there were further damaging allegations - none of them suggesting real corruption, but all adding to the overall image of sleaze - that Aitken had procured prostitutes for Arabs, and that while minister for defence procurement, he had concealed his links with a Middle Eastern arms company involved in an arms deal between the Lebanese government and Britain. Then he was accused of being financially dependent on his Arab contacts, including the son of the Saudi king. It has been speculated that Aitken was only put in the Ministry of Defence because Arabs objected to having Malcolm Rifkind, a Jew, as the more senior Secretary of State for Defence. "Put Jonathan in defence," one is supposed to have told another senior politician, "or you can kiss the [defence] contracts goodbye."

Investigators and intelligence officials have also suggested Aitken's Arab backers were hoping to see 'their man' installed in 10 Downing Street as Prime Minister, battling for their interests on the international stage.

The whole saga became a morass of claim and counter-claim. The Guardian and their co-defendants, the investigative current-affairs program World in Action, made further allegations about Aitken's involvement in arms companies during the 1980s in December 1995, to which Aitken responded with fury.

But slowly, the defendant's case solidified. They discovered Aitken had admitted he had spoken with one of the most senior Saudis during his stay at the hotel (despite previously denying doing so) to a senior Tory party official during an internal enquiry into the Guardian's claims.

The defendants had another crucial piece of evidence. They obtained a record of all the phone calls made from his hotel room on the crucial morning in question, and discovered he had rung the Hotel Bristol in the Swiss village of Villars, where his young daughter Victoria was attending school. Guardian investigators were jubilant - Aitken could only have been ringing his wife Lolicia (who was visiting Victoria) at the time she was supposed to be in Paris paying his hotel bill. They thought they had their proof.

But Aitken is a wily character. He suddenly introduced his mother-in-law into his story, claiming she had been sharing a room with his wife Lolicia and while she had travelled on to France her mother had stayed-on in the room. He had been chatting with her on the phone, he said. How could the defendants possibly disprove his new claim? The Hotel Bristol had been closed down since 1993.

In desperation Owen Boycott, a Guardian investigative journalist, flew out to Switzerland and drove to the abandoned Hotel Bristol in the village of Villars. He found the hotel closed and shuttered, with a ageing caretaker pottering around. The old man disclosed there were boxes of hotel records still sitting in the basement. Boycott rolled up his sleeves and spent four days reading through endless receipts and files before he struck gold.

Boycott found Lolicia's bill for a double room, shared with her daughter Victoria for one night. However on the crucial night in question Boycott discovered Lolicia had asked for a reduction of 80 Swiss francs on the normal room rate "because of single occupancy". For a wealthy man with two huge homes, those 80 francs have cost Aitken dearly. The reduction proved there was no mother-in-law staying with Lolicia. Aitken had lied - he had not spoken to her. His story was crumbling.

Then Valerie Scott, Aitken's former secretary, destroyed another element of his story - that the Ritz bill was paid in cash as his wife could not use credit cards because of her dyslexia. "Dyslexia?!" said Scott. "I used to follow Lolicia around shops while she wrote cheques and signed credit cards galore!" Another round to the investigators.

Owen Boycott in Switzerland further tightened the screws when he discovered further discrepancies in Aitken's story. The MP had claimed his wife could or did not use credit cards. But her bill at the Hotel Bristol was paid in full with her personal American Express card, the existence of which was not known before. A subpoena was issued and Lolicia's Amex records for that month were delivered to the Guardian. They showed she had rented a VW Golf during her stay at the hotel, and had hired the car from Geneva airport, which meant Lolicia had arrived in Switzerland by air. A week before this discovery, Aitken had sworn a statement that Lolicia and Victoria had travelled to Geneva on the train. Another lie.

Investigators began enquiring about passengers on the flights into Geneva international airport over the weekend in question. A report from a British Airways investigator proved the crucial piece of evidence against Aitken; it showed that Lolicia Aitken returned the hired car in Geneva two hours after she was supposed to have paid-off the cashier at the Ritz in Paris. Aitken's case against the Guardian collapsed. The newspaper headlines the following day must have been the final indignity: "He lied and lied and lied", said one, "Jail him", was the even-more succinct headline on the front page of the mass-market Daily Mirror.

"Aitken's own downfall was caused by a cover-up, a lie about a weekend in Paris in 1993," said a front page editorial in the Guardian after the collapse of the case against the newspaper. "We still do not know why it was so vital that he should have lied so doggedly and consistently about that weekend, but it was emphatically the lie, not the trip, that finished him."

"That initial lie ensnared not only him, but his family, for it was vital to Aitken to be able to pretend that his wife paid his bill at the Ritz Hotel in Paris. In fact, as we were eventually able to prove, Mrs Aitken spent the weekend in Switzerland with their daughter Victoria. Thus was Aitken's 17-year-old child also sucked into an ever more desperate conspiracy. It would be inhuman not to feel sympathy for the Aitken family as they contemplate the wreckage of their lives. But it is hard to feel much compassion for a man who would send in his own daughter to tell lies on oath - a serious criminal offence which could even have cost her her liberty - to save his own skin. Such behaviour in any father, never mind a Privy Counsellor, is repulsive. That is why they police should send for the court papers with some urgency."

Even if Aitken is now forced to leave the 'gatekeeping business', there are plenty more businessmen waiting to take his place. The only requirement appears to be a wide circle of powerful friends, as most existing gatekeepers seem to be well acquainted. Another contact of Aitken's is a wealthy Middle Eastern businessman who is equally at ease in London or Damascus: the Syrian businessman Wafic Said, who first met Aitken when the disgraced MP went to the Middle East for the Slater Walker company. Aitken later persuaded Said to invest in Aitken's banking company, Aitken Hume. Said may also be termed a crucial gatekeeper; by the mid 1980s -

when a huge £20 billion arms negotiation was underway - he was an important intermediary between the Saudis and the British government. It is said his influence won the day for British Aerospace in the face of competition from French armaments concerns. But that Said is a wealthy man is not in dispute. In 1996 he offered to donate £20 million to Oxford University to set up a world-class business school. When in Britain, Said lives in either his £9 million apartment in Eaton Square or his 3,000 acre estate in Oxfordshire. His wealth is founded upon his knowledge of the West and his excellent relationships with the Saudi royal family's inner circle. There are many critical things which may be said about the trade of the international fixers, but one comment is indisputable: it is lucrative work.

Chapter Seven

ILL-GOTTEN GAINS

"Where your treasure is, there will your heart be also"
St Matthew's Gospel (6:21)

THE LANGUAGE of corruption is colloquial and expressive: sweetening, dashing, brown envelopes, backhanders, suborn, bungs, drops, baksheesh. Most of us recognise that these terms refer to bribes and graft, where a monetary reward is involved.

But does hospitality ever amount to a bribe? What about 'jobs for the boys'? Can such schemes represent payment for favours and if they do, is there anything wrong or immoral?

The payment of a large sum of cash to an elected official in return for the award of a lucrative contract would be identified by most observers as clearly corrupt. When a former politician is awarded a senior position within a company he previously dealt with in government, the public are rightly suspicious, but this is allowed subject to certain time restrictions.

Public office can lead to private gain. Yet bribes are not always obvious. They do not always consist of brown envelopes changing hands under restaurant tables. Corruption also includes 'sleazy' dealing, mutual back-scratching, patronage and favouritism. The reader must decide what is right and what is wrong, for often the law cannot help.

How do we define the morality of corruption? One hundred people may provide one hundred differing interpretations.

In a submission to Lord Nolan's Committee on Standards in Public Life, the British Institute of Business Ethics provided a three-part formula to assist a recipient in deciding where the line is to be drawn between an acceptable present or a bribe: the 'sleep well factor' - would acceptance keep the recipient awake at night?; newspaper reports - would the recipient mind seeing the circumstances reported in a newspaper?; standard of living - would acceptance alter the recipients' standard of living?

These issues arose when Peter Davis, paid £80,000 a year as the UK national lottery regulator, Oflot, came under criticism in 1996 for accepting hospitality from G-Tech, a company with a 22% stake in Camelot, the consortium which succeeded in the contest to run the British national lottery.

In October 1994, Davis made a tour of G-Tech's US operations, after the contract had been won by Camelot, but other contracts such as scratch-cards, were still open to decision. Guidelines were available from the Department of National Heritage about the dangers inherent in accepting hospitality, but Davis was a guest at the Long Island home of a G-Tech director, whose wife was a friend of Davis' wife. In addition, Davis was transported around during his tour by G-Tech aircraft and G-Tech limousines.

Responding to the adverse publicity, Davis claimed that using such facilities formed the only means open to him to cover the distances involved in his tour. He said he had privately declared the hospitality to his civil service bosses, but the story illustrates how difficult it is to avoid suspicion.

In November 1996 Davis was publicly criticised by a number of MPs for his 'dilatory' and 'unimaginative' approach to his job. Davis was also criticised by the Commons Public Accounts Committee for failing to keep rigorous checks on Camelot.

These attacks followed an official study by the National Audit Office which showed that of 21 checks devised by Oflot to regulate Camelot, only one had been implemented.

Alan Williams, Labour MP for Swansea West, said the report expressed 'administrative incompetence', going on to say that Davis's period at Oflot had been a period of "quite inadequate protection of the public interest". Mr Davis was also criticised for failing to use his powers to allow Sir John Bourn, Comptroller and Auditor General, to inspect Camelot's accounts. When asked to make its records available by the National Audit Office, Camelot had refused.

Belatedly Davis seemed to have got the message. After Labour won the General Election he asked the Heritage Secretary, Chris Smith, for 'stronger teeth' to deal with breaches of guidelines. He said any fines would have to be large to reflect the fact that the lottery turned over £5billion a year.

IN SINGAPORE surveys of Asian business suggest a lack of corruption in the city state where Senior Minister, Lee Kuan Yew, seen by many as the founder of modern Singapore, prides himself on the state's corruption-free government. Lee held office for 31 years before surrendering executive power in 1990 to Prime Minister Goh Chok Tong. But during 1996 there were the first signs of public discontent at the perks enjoyed by leading figures. Salaries enjoyed by Singapore officials are high (Lee himself receives a salary of $1.3 million) and other ministers are rewarded accordingly.

Many supporters of the high salaries argue that well-remunerated officers are immunised against bribery. The focus for public and official discontent was discounts offered by developers of luxury condominiums in Singapore. During the five years prior to 1996, Singapore property values had risen sharply, some by more than 150%. In an attempt to rein in the market the Singapore Government imposed a capital gains tax on properties sold after less than three years, providing a strong disincentive to the speculators.

A matter of days after this measure was announced, Lee went before Parliament with his son, the deputy prime minister, Lee Hsien Loong, to say that both of them had been granted discounts by a developer in a 'soft launch' operation. Under a 'soft launch', developers make properties available to associates or celebrities before the properties are marketed to the general public, with the potential for instant profit once the market is opened up. Lee and his wife bought two units at a cost of £5 million, receiving a discount approaching £200,000.

Lee was reportedly 'astonished' these purchases should be questioned, explaining that he expected and accepted discount from his tailor and shoemaker. "It is an unfair and unequal world," he said candidly. "There are discounts for him but not for the ordinary person, so that's the way it is," said opposition politician Ben Jeyaretnam in disgust. After a public outcry, Lee donated the value of the discount to charity.

IN 1994, US Senate and House of Representatives officials agreed to a review of the rules on perks to answer critics. As a result, gifts of any value were banned for House members and a gift acceptance limit of $50 was imposed upon Senators. Also forbidden by the legislation were golf and skiing trips where businesses paid the bills. Even lunch and dinner invitations are excluded unless the person making the invitation is a relative, friend or represents a charitable organisation. The effect on restaurants near to Congress has been crippling.

While still President-elect in December 1992 Bill Clinton vowed to clean up sleaze. He banned members of the team responsible for his transition into the Oval Office from becoming involved in public matters where they might have a financial interest. However, Mike Espy, Secretary of Agriculture, resigned in 1994 after accusations he accepted favours - in the form of sporting tickets and transport - from the largest chicken producer in the USA, Tyson Food Corporation. Commenting upon the matter, The Wall Street Journal said the affair illustrated, "the larger story now of people who are unable to recognise any line between the realms of private and public life."

There is clear public unease with the grey areas where the line between propriety and impropriety is blurred. Nobody would deny a public official the right to modest refreshment while conducting official business. The problems arise when the term 'modest' is wilfully misinterpreted.

The Hong Kong government has taken a strong line in the fight against corruption since 1974 and the foundation of its Independent Commission Against Corruption (discussed in more detail later). Legislation there to combat sleaze is powerful, but even then it is recognised there are 'grey' activities.

The Hong Kong Civil Service provides information, advice and a set of rules in a circular entitled 'Conflict of Interest'. The ICAC also has what it calls the capacity test, asking the simple question: "Would that advantage have been offered to me if I were not holding my present official position?" If the answer is 'no' then the offer should be viewed with suspicion.

WHERE a public official makes a private gain connected, however tenuously, to his or her public duty, the electorate suspects the worst and the same can be said about political parties. If donors to a political party accrue some advantage when that party is in government, suspicions are aroused and not easily allayed.

In Britain certain policies of the last Conservative government attracted allegations of political back-scratching and patronage which are mirrored in other developed nations.

The word Quango is an acronym for Quasi-Autonomous Non-Governmental Organisation. The word, never, officially recognised by the Tories (who prefer the title EGO - Extra Governmental Organisation), describes organisations not part of the Civil Service, but funded by the taxpayer. Such organisations are entirely within the sphere of influence of a government Minister but there is little consultation as to whether they are necessary or how they should be operated. As such, they are vehicles for patronage for rewarding the politically faithful and ensuring the 'right' (depending on which side of the fence one sits) political bias.

The use of Quangos for the purpose of patronage is not new. The Labour Party of the 1970s employed the same system with one crucial difference. Then Quangos were almost entirely advisory bodies with little or no spending powers. Now they spend approximately £60 billion per year. It will be interesting to see whether the new Labour government reins in their power.

Quangos range in size from boards of school governors to district health authorities and Training and Enterprise Councils (TECs). The Medical Research Council, London Tourist Board and the Takeover Panel also fall into this category. In 1994 there were 5,521 that fell under the Quango definition in that members were appointed, rather than elected, and the organisations were publicly funded. The Government's definition was tighter, excluding for example hospital trust boards, and this made it appear that the number had been reduced to just 1,389, fulfilling a previous promise.

Labour MPs Michael Meacher and Peter Kilfoyle have both expressed interest in the subject of Quangos and appointees to them, Meacher drawing attention to possible links between party donations and Quango appointments. He has drawn attention to 20 such organisations where chairmen are associated to Tory party donors. A Labour party document 'Quangos and Donations to the Tory Party' makes similar allegations, as do other studies. But the real concern is that appointees to Quangos might be able to influence investment and regulation in areas where they have other commercial interests.

IF POLITICAL appointees to Quangos may be seen as 'keeping it in the family' as far as patronage is concerned, then the same phrase certainly rings true when one considers favouritism in the European Commission. In 1996 a review of recruitment procedures was initiated after concern was expressed about the methods used to allocate jobs. A new word was coined - 'parachutisme' - where incoming commissioners bring with them friends and political allies who secure key jobs in the bureaucratic system.

Once in a job at Brussels, there is job security, a high salary and low taxes. A system of bonuses adds to basic pay. In November 1996, Erkki Liikonen, a Finnish commissioner, began the task of reforming job allocation by listing hundreds of officials in Brussels who had by-passed the normal channels of recruitment. His work was highly unpopular among some staff.

Patronage and favouritism are not always seen as corrupt or even 'sleazy', particularly from the perspective of those who benefit. Spiro Agnew, Vice President of the United States, was forced to resign in 1973 because of sleaze allegations. After plea bargaining, Agnew was allowed to plead 'no contest' to a single charge of tax evasion which emanated from payments received in 1967 while he was Governor of Maryland. Agnew claimed the alleged bribes were campaign contributions, claiming the normal practice in Maryland was to give public contracts to friends rather than political rivals, a practice which he obviously saw as perfectly acceptable.

A GOOD starting point when examining how money is secretly organised, moved and banked for political ends is the administration of Richard Milhous Nixon, US President during Agnew's Vice Presidency. Nixon is synonymous with the Watergate Affair, which had its simple origins in the arrest on 17th June 1972 of five men burgling the Democratic National Committee Headquarters at the Watergate complex in Washington. Thus began an investigation which led right into the Nixon administration, to the conviction and imprisonment of Nixon aides and the eventual resignation of Nixon himself as President.

Part of the ensuing investigation focused upon identifying sources of funding for the Watergate break-in and other illegal actions. In July 1973 Watergate Special Prosecutor Archibald Cox announced he had evidence that American Airlines had made an illegal $55,000 contribution to the Campaign to Re-elect the President (CREEP). As a result of a request from Cox that other corporations voluntarily disclose illegal contributions and a law suit brought against CREEP by the pressure group Common Cause, asking that all corporate contributions be revealed, 18 corporations were convicted of violating federal electoral laws.

Nixon had already had a close shave over secret campaign contributions, prior to the Watergate investigation when press reports in March 1972 alleged a $400,000 contribution had been made by International Telephone and Telegraph Corporation, (ITT) as a secret quid pro quo for the Nixon administration's favourable treatment of ITT during an anti-trust legal action. Nixon's opponents quoted an ITT lobbyist, Dita Beard, as confirming this.

But Nixon did not let this near-miss divert him. He was not going to miss re-election for lack of funds and had planned fund-raising activities for his second term during his first term of office. There was $1.6 remaining from the 1968 election war chest and this was retained as a secret political fund. But in April 1972 the Federal Election Campaign Act came into force, which meant campaign contributions and expenditures would have to be declared with contributors identified.

Under the legislation prior to April 1972, contributions to nominated candidates had to be identified, but those to candidates not formally nominated did not. As Nixon was only a candidate for nomination, any cash received prior to April 1972 did not have to be accounted for and as a result there was a welter of donations. However, one thing was the same under both the old law and the new - corporate contributions were illegal.

It is not possible here to detail all the schemes that were used by corporations to help CREEP and only the scheme adopted by the Gulf Oil Corporation will be examined. Gulf executives apparently became increasingly worried in the late 1950s about the encroachment by the Government towards the oil industry and as a result decided to launder and distribute corporate funds to politicians in an attempt to redress the balance. The chosen vehicle was Bahamas Exploration, an almost dormant Gulf subsidiary based in Nassau. From 1959 onwards its budget multiplied dramatically as it became the hub of an illegal funding operation.

William Viglia was responsible for accounting at several Bahamian subsidiaries, including Bahamas Exploration. He was instructed to open several bank accounts in the Bahamas to receive Gulf funds and money was transferred to the Bahamas to be taken in envelopes to Claude Wild, the head of the Gulf Government Relations office in Washington.

The court was told: "Viglia ... never ... [came] to Wild's office ... no records were maintained ...when Wild needed funds he telephoned Viglia and Viglia delivered the cash ... Wild and Viglia met at various points throughout the United States but never in a Gulf Office" - [Securities and Exchange Commission, Plaintiff v Gulf Oil Corporation, Claude C Wild Jr, Defendant].

Wild organised a team of carriers to distribute the cash, although he personally handled nearly all payments to candidates for national office. The only criterion for the distribution of the funds was that the money had to be spent in the general interest of Gulf and the oil industry.

CREEP received $100,000 in illegal funds from Gulf. There was no reliable evidence that the recipients of this money knew that it was from a corporate source and therefore illegal.

Corporate contributions are once again an issue in US politics because of the work of Political Action Committees (which were ruled to be legal by the Federal Election Commission in 1975, a decision upheld by the Supreme Court in 1976), but there is a greater degree of transparency and therefore greater public ease. Indeed, there are those who have difficulty in seeing why corporate contributions should ever have been criminalised as, unlike bribes for specific favours, corporate contributions usually have more general and less identifiable goals.

IN FRANCE, secret funding of political activity seems to be inextricably linked with personal enrichment. In September 1994 Gerard Languet, Minister of Industry and Foreign Trade, was involved in two scandals, one involving the building of an undervalued house for himself and the other the secret funding of the Republican Party. Sections of French society have tended to view the secret funding of political activity as the price that must be paid for the existence of political parties in a democratic system.

Following the election of a French President, it is common for them to pass an Amnesty nullifying minor offences. Following the 1988 presidential election, the amnesty law pardoned almost all election offences. This was, however, followed by a second amnesty law in 1990, which carried a paragraph stating: "Except if the offender obtains personal enrichment, all breaches of the law committed before, 15th June, 1989, in relation to the direct or indirect funding of election campaigns or political parties or groups, are amnestied except those offences committed by a person invested with a national parliamentary mandate."

The growing public feeling that French politicians are becoming increasingly corrupt, has been fuelled by a number of political scandals culminating in the Carrignon affair and the Séguin Law against corruption, passed in December, 1994. The Séguin Law tightened controls in relation to the awards of public contracts, the funding of political parties by business and aimed to introduce greater oversight of matters involving public funds.

The passing of the act was predicated by the imprisonment of Alain Carrignon in October 1994. Carrignon had been a Minister for Communications in the Government of Edouard Balladur and had resigned following allegations of corrupt practice while mayor of Grenoble. Carrignon was actually imprisoned by the investigating magistrate to prevent destruction of evidence following allegations he had received lucrative 'advantages' from firms seeking public contracts. The advantages included the use of a luxury flat, travel facilities and the provision of subsidised electoral publicity.

Two other French politicians had fled the country while under investigation for misconduct. In early 1991, Jean Michel Boucheron, Mayor of Angoulême, was charged with corruption and fraud and subsequently fled to Buenos Aires. He was accused of receiving benefit from public contracts through an elaborate system of forged invoices provided by firms that were awarded the business.

Jacques Medécin, political boss of Nice in the 1980s, was accused of fraud by opposition politicians in 1989, and by author Graham Greene, and fled to Uruguay. Investigations led to his imprisonment following extradition; the same investigations revealed Medécin had property holdings in the USA, secret overseas bank accounts and shareholdings abroad.

THERE IS a great difference between public officials taking favours for the award of contracts, and leaders of countries systematically looting the national economy. The Commission on Good Government set up after Ferdinand Marcos was deposed in The Philippines in 1986 is still trying to recover national assets he expropriated - between $3 billion and $7 billion.

Imelda Marcos, the former first lady of The Philippines, claims her late husband, who died in 1989, actually supported The Philippines economy from his own finances, using wealth derived from the discovery of war booty hidden by the Japanese during the Second World War - booty which became known as Yamashitas Gold.

However Sterling Seagrave, the author of the book, 'The Marcos Dynasty', lists a catalogue of skulduggery. "Among journalists, it was generally understood that some of the (Ferdinand) Marcos wealth came from the crooked sale of import licences, from countless murky business deals, from his tobacco monopoly, from multinational kickbacks, from smuggling and racketeering with Chinese syndicates and Japanese Yakuza, from deals with American mobsters, and from a lion's share of Philippine gambling proceeds," said Seagrave.

"A large part certainly came from the US government in the form of misdirected aid funds, detoured war reparations, inflated military base rent, side-tracked World Bank and IMF millions and secret grants made by the White House as a means of high level bribery. Another sizeable portion came from confiscating the wealth of others and seizing businesses and properties."

The implications are that there was hardly an area of The Philippines economy from which Marcos was not drawing off a profit. But where did all this wealth go? In the wake of the 1986 uprising, a Greek aide of Imelda Marcos was caught trying to smuggle 20 suitcases of rubies and diamonds out of Manila. These gems were valued at $6 million. A second hoard was found at the Marcos' palace and was valued at $300,000.

The Marcos's fled from The Philippines to Hawaii and upon arrival, claimed they were poverty-stricken. American Custom and Immigration Officers, however, found $4 million in cash, a gold crown, three tiaras, 60 pearl necklaces, 35 rings and a $1 million emerald necklace in their luggage. Apart from this readily portable wealth, it is alleged millions were (and possibly still are) stashed in secret bank accounts in Switzerland.

DESPITE its reputation, Switzerland is now no longer the haven of choice for the $1,500 billion per year of grey money circulating the globe. This money, the profits from organised crime, bribes, tax evasion, arms and drug dealing gravitates towards those countries offering secrecy and ease of access but since 1989, Switzerland has had stronger controls.

In relation to money laundering arising out of crime, other havens are more popular including the Channel Islands, the Cayman Islands, the Seychelles, Ireland, Belgium, Andorra, Uruguay and the Isle of Man.

As in the Medécin case, referred to above, corporate structures may be used in conjunction with discreet banking arrangements to conceal ownership of assets and to facilitate pay offs. Nominee companies may be used to hold assets or conduct transactions. Companies may be incorporated into a maze of cross-shareholdings with nominee shareholders and trusts. One or more of these legal entities may be domiciled in a tax haven, creating a barrier to investigation. Finally, fictitious transactions involving the raising of invoices, fictitious sources of revenue and inter company loans may be used to disguise slush funds.

The West was amazed when it was revealed Saddam Hussein of Iraq had huge investments in the west, buried beneath corporate blankets and front men, some of them his own family members. These investments were located, in part, by Kroll Associates, a private investigation agency hired by the Kuwaiti government to locate Hussein's riches following the Gulf War.

The agency, staffed by ex-FBI agents, accountants, economists and business experts, specialises in financial investigations. Kroll revealed in March 1991 that using a Panamanian registered holding company called Montana Management, Hussein had allegedly succeeded in investing $34 million in an 8.4% holding in Hachette, a large media company publishing such well-known women's magazines as Elle and Woman's Day. In a similar vein Kroll has also tracked down funds allegedly siphoned out of the Philippines by Ferdinand Marcos and money originating from the regime of Jean Claude Duvalier in Haiti.

As money laundering has become more sophisticated, the means of dismantling the infrastructure of corruption has become more sophisticated and expensive. Kroll, Pinkertons and many other similar firms, employed discreetly to counter corruption, are tapping into a multi-million pound business.

Chapter Eight

RISK
AREAS

"I can resist everything except temptation"
Oscar Wilde (Lady Windermere's Fan)

OPEN A newspaper anywhere in the world and you will see allegations of 'sleaze'. If the media are tenacious, perhaps they will boldly allege outright corruption.

The allegations are levelled at politicians, heads of states, and entire regimes. But corruption and misconduct need an environment in which to grow, a culture medium if you will, and it is these 'vulnerable' areas which are the subject of this chapter.

As already stated, not all conduct which attracts unfavourable attention and comment is corrupt in the legal sense of the word, but it may harm democracy by damaging public confidence in the democratic system. The number of areas in public life where undue influence may be exercised is vast and broad generalisations must be made. However, two areas deserve chapters of their own: organised crime, and the arms trade, both of which are discussed later.

Aside from these two specific areas, influence may be brought to bear in the areas of: a) the seeking of contracts, permissions, concessions and subsidies from government; b) the introduction or reform of legislation or procedures; c) the non enforcement of legislation or procedures by public officials; d) and the conduct of foreign relations

In 1992, an investigation by Antonio di Pietro and a 'clean hands' pool of magistrates in Italy began quietly. Mario Chiesa, socialist director of a nursing home in Milan was charged with extorting a £2,700 kickback for the award of a cleaning contract for the home. Subsequent investigations began to unearth a huge 'iceberg of influence' throughout Italy, through which contracts were directed to the 'right people'.

There was a wave of arrests by the 'clean pool' team (dubbed 'Tangentopoli' or 'Bribesville' by the Italian press) and a second wave followed, targeting another network of public sector managers.

The first to be arrested was Lorenzo Necci, head of the state railway company, and until then regarded as a possible Government super-minister with oversight of transport and public works contracts. Evidence gathered by the investigating magistrates suggested Necci was involved in a multi-billion lire scheme to cream off money from state contracts. Press reports alleged Necci had admitted to accepting $8,000 per month in kickbacks from potential contractors.

Despite the efforts of the 'clean hands pool', with thousands of arrests, interviews and endless court proceedings, only one person, a former Milan city councillor, Walter Armanini, has been convicted and jailed - hardly a deterrent.

Tender rigging or fixing has become a European-wide issue according to Per Brix Knudsen, director of the European Commission's anti-fraud co-ordination unit. In his view public procurement and the tendering for public contracts are becoming the target of organised fraudsters willing to bribe. The temptations are obvious and the potential rewards immense.

However, early in 1997, the French courts took what may be cynically called an understanding view of the practicalities of conducting business in the public sector. In a case before the Cour de Cassation, France's supreme court, Serge Crasnianski, head of a photographic equipment firm, KIS, was alleged to have bribed the son-in-law of a former minister of trade, Michel Noir, in return for tax concessions.

The Cour de Cassation ruled that Crasnianski should not have been convicted in the lower courts of the offence of misuse of company funds because the bribe secured a large return for the company, overturning an earlier ruling in 1992 that using corporate money for any illegal purpose was an abuse.

Prior to this later ruling, the misuse of funds charge had been the preferred option of prosecutors, who felt the alternative charges - corruption or peddling influence - were difficult to prove, particularly with their requirement to demonstrate a definite link between the bribe and the award of a contract or grant of a favour. In making its ruling, it appeared the Cour de Cassation recognised the temptations faced by businessmen pushing for concessions and contracts. With such an understanding stance taken by the French Court and the seeming inability of the Italian courts to capitalise upon investigations widely supported by the Italian public, it is no wonder businessmen are still corrupting those in the public sector.

SO WHAT are the safeguards put in place to ensure probity in the award of contracts, permissions and concessions? The basis of most systems is competition. This is supposed to ensure equality in that all those who are capable are given a fair and equal opportunity. It is also thought to be economic because the best value is achieved. Competitive tendering is most often seen as the answer.

Guidelines for effective tendering systems usually incorporate certain inherent features: the preparation of detailed information as to what is required from a supplier or conversely, what is on offer to a purchaser; details of rights to be conferred and/or obligations imposed upon prospective bidders; security of bids made with sealed tenders opened in the presence of witnesses at a given time; oversight of the procedures by a number of persons rather than authority being given to one - the higher the values at stake, the greater the number of overseers; and, preparation of objective criteria for the assessment of bids, preferably before offers are invited.

There are many variations upon these themes and, unfortunately, many methods used to frustrate competitive tenders. The first is the argument that competitive tendering is an expensive and time consuming business and, where speed is vital, it can be safely ignored by direct negotiation with those who have established track records.

If competitive tendering is to be used, the following are some examples of methods used to frustrate it: leakage of information as to selection criteria or competitors' bids; the drawing up of tender specifications to favour one party to the process, to the effective exclusion of all others; and arguments for favouring suppliers/purchasers on the grounds of promoting the local economy through re-investment of profits or spin off development.

Most of these methods are capable of innocent interpretation because there will be occasions when these methods would be used for right and proper reasons: speed, public savings, compensation of a bidder acting in good faith who has been misled unintentionally. What cannot be known is what may be happening out of the public gaze.

On those occasions when changes to the specification, contracts, for example, are undertaken quite properly, nothing is happening below the surface. But where variations are made for corrupt reasons, much may be happening. The problem is how does the public differentiate? How can we tell? There is no ideal solution, but transparency in the award of public contracts would be a crucial first step.

Several UK privatisations have attracted adverse comment and allegations of cosy dealings with favoured purchasers even though no corruption was apparent. Of the sale of Her Majesty's Stationery Office to a group made up of Electra Investment Trust and bankers Robert Fleming, Labour public services spokesman Derek Foster claimed: "The deal was a farce. The company was sold at a knock down price to Tory donors."

His allegations were based upon the fact that Electra Investment Trust and Robert Fleming, the investment bank, have together contributed nearly £600,000 to the Conservative Party in recent years. Lord King, a former cabinet minister, is on Electra's board and a former Tory Chief Whip, Tim Renton, is employed by Robert Fleming as a parliamentary consultant.

So what of the 'knock down price'? Suspicions were fuelled as the sale price - £54 million - was a third of the forecast figure. But those who allege misconduct and preferential treatment should also consider the state of the business - HMSO - which was described as being in a 'state of chaos' with 'holes' in its accounts, properties unaccounted for and with warehouses crammed with useless stationery.

Fourteen bids had been made, ranging up to £175 million, with four consortia eventually shortlisted: Mercury Asset Management, Hambros, Electra Fleming and NatWest Ventures. As a result of inspections made, the final bids made by each of the shortlisted companies was lower than the original.

The eventual winner, Electra Fleming bid in the region of £70 million. Where criticism has been levelled, however, is that having secured preferred bidder status, another 20% reduction in price was directly negotiated. The disparity between original estimates and final bids is partially explained by the state of the business, but doubts lingered and the National Audit office quite rightly announced it would be investigating.

The sale of Armed Forces married quarters for £1.66 billion suggested a further lack of transparency. The deal was concluded with a Japanese backed firm, but members of the House of Commons Defence Committee who questioned representatives of the purchaser, Annington Homes, in November 1996 were astonished after they were initially denied names of those involved in the project. Annington Homes is a consortium, with 75% owned by the Japanese Nomura International and including participants such as The Royal Bank of Scotland and Abbey National.

MPs learnt that although the MoD had sold 57,400 properties to Annington Homes, the real owner was Annington Property Limited. The names of the directors of this company were supplied to the committee only after Menzies Campbell MP strongly rebuked Guy Hands, the managing director of Nomura International. The Committee, with a Conservative majority, said it could endorse neither the principle of the sale nor the choice of buyer made by the Ministry of Defence. At the time political opponents of the sale and housing analysts had said the £1.66 billion price tag was too low because of the potentially huge profits to be made.

TURNING to the dangers of influence being exerted by the introduction or reform of legislation, President Clinton's fund-raisers in the run up to the 1996 US election also stand accused of a lack of judgement. Seventeen of America's top bankers met with the President at the White House in the presence of the Administration's chief banking regulator, Eugene Ludwig and political operators seeking donations to the Democratic Campaign war chest. "It's about as close to a quid pro quo as we are likely to see," said Ellen Miller, director of Public Campaign, a non partisan group calling for the reform of political financing.

Republicans complained that inviting the bankers to a political event in the White House, where fundraising is illegal, was unethical - at the very least. Even Eugene Ludwig, via a spokeswoman, admitted he felt the gathering had been inappropriate, believing it to be a group of bankers meeting to discuss banking legislation. He did not know the Democratic Committee had been invited, "If he had, he would not have gone.", the spokeswoman said.

John McCain, a Republican Senator who co-sponsored a Bill to reform campaign finance, to call for the appointment of an independent counsel to investigate Democratic fundraising. Other Republicans, however, rightly feared such a call could backfire by drawing attention to their own party's reliance upon large corporate donors.

For the 1996 election campaign, Bill Clinton and the Democratic National Committee raised $229 million, while Bob Dole and the Republican National Committee raised $312 million. It is difficult to correlate corporate political donations with legislative or regulatory benefit, but almost inevitably, those companies involved in politically sensitive or heavily regulated sectors of business have contributed most to the two major US political parties in recent years.

The largest corporate donor to the Republican National Committee was Philip Morris, the tobacco company, which gave $2.5 million between 1st January 1995 and 25th November 1996. Other tobacco companies were also generous: RJR Nabisco gave $1.15 million; Brown and Williamson $635,000; United States Tobacco $539,000. Tobacco interests were fighting a battle on two fronts to protect their activities; firstly against a Justice Department investigation into whether the industry misled Congress by suppressing evidence proving tobacco is addictive and secondly to convince the Food and Drug Administration not to regulate tobacco as a drug. The level of political spending by tobacco companies has more then doubled since 1993, as presidential support has grown for anti-smoking objectives.

In attacking tobacco interests, the Democrats walk a fine line. For while anti-smoking measures win votes, the party relies heavily on tobacco state votes and tobacco money. The opposition to anti-smoking measures also claim that by taking on one special interest group, the Democrats are cosying up to another: trial lawyers who would gain enormously from liability suits brought against cigarette manufacturers. Coincidentally, trial lawyers are the biggest single interest contributors to the Democratic Party. Between January and September 1995, they donated $2.5 million to the Clinton Campaign.

Others sought to influence political views in the United States during the run-up to the 1996 presidential election. Long distance telecommunications companies led by AT&T and MCI secured a change to the telecommunications bill which threatened to allow regional telephone companies to enter the long distance market without giving up their own local monopolies. MCI made donations of approximately $750,000, much of the money being expended in the latter half of 1995, while the telecommunications bill was passing through Congress.

Oil and gas companies spent money seeking to combat tougher environmental legislation and the threat of a tax on energy. The Canadian based Seagram distillery group gave $650,000 to the Republicans and $270,000 to the Democrats seeking to deflect political attacks following its decision to break the voluntary ban on advertising spirits on television.

THERE IS, of course, a world of difference between attempting to influence the drawing-up of legislation and the disregard for the enforcement of rules by public officials in return for favours. Our third risk area is exemplified by the case of Michael Allcock, a senior British Inland Revenue official, who was convicted in February 1997 of taking bribes and sentenced to five years in prison.

Allcock had been the head of Inland Revenue Special Office 2, one of the Special Office Units which targeted the rich and famous, including wealthy foreign businessmen, pop stars and celebrities. The unit which Allcock headed was responsible for recovering hundreds of millions of pounds in back tax from wealthy individuals who often had no tax identity and were known to the Inland Revenue as 'ghosts'. As a natural progression, the Special Office staff became known in the slang of the Inland Revenue as 'Ghostbusters'.

However, Allcock, the top 'Ghostbuster' was corrupted by those he should have been pursuing. An Old Bailey court accepted his high levels of spending on hotels, holidays, clothes, home improvements and cars, had not been paid for with inherited wealth, but from payments both in cash and kind from his wealthy paymasters. In return they received favourable tax settlements and protection from further inquiry. Allcock accepted the services of a prostitute, who later became his mistress, a Concorde trip to New York and Bermuda with his wife and family and cash bribes, of which £155,000 was traced to bank accounts under his control. It was suspected this cash represented only a portion of they total wealth received by Allcock, who had the power to settle multi-million pound sums without recourse to any other authority within the Inland Revenue.

Despite his ostentatious lifestyle, Allcock was caught completely by accident. A different branch of the Inland Revenue investigating a businessman found an entry in an accountants' file belonging to a wealthy Arab, which referred to 'Allcock' and the word 'payoff'. Following the case, several of Allcock's colleagues faced internal disciplinary inquiries.

Allcock argued throughout his trial that his department knew he regularly accepted lavish hospitality during the course of his work and that he and his staff were allowed airline tickets and accommodation at the expense of those they targeted. Following discovery of Allcock's wrongdoing, Revenue supervisory procedures were overhauled, restricting the opportunities for abusing the system. Inspectors were required to decline all but the most petty gifts and hospitality and foreign travel was restricted and never accepted at the expense of a suspected tax evader.

WHEREVER there is regulation and potential for enforcement, so there is potential for corruption of officers. Just as Allcock lived the high life by abusing his official position, so there are others who avoid restrictions being placed upon their enjoyment of the high life by paying officials not to regulate them.

Young wealthy Iranians enjoy a fabulous life of parties and music in Teheran while the country lies under the restrictions of Islamic Law. The 'sharia', as it is called, advocates death (by stoning) of women found guilty of adultery. Alcohol, Western music and satellite television are all banned, but the wealthy find their way around such restrictions by paying off corrupt policemen.

Similarly, exemption may be purchased from the compulsory two year military service in Iran, which is usually spent living in the field, patrolling sensitive border areas. The going rate for such exemption is about £11,000, paid to corrupt officials. Wherever there is regulation there is potential for corruption, even in a strict Islamic nation.

Examination of the fourth risk area - the conduct of foreign relations - moves the analysis into a high stakes realm of trade wars, trade deals, human rights, economic aid and even armed conflict. The prospect of foreign donors to political parties influencing British foreign policy was raised by the case of Mohammed Hashemi, a wealthy businessman under investigation by the Serious Fraud Office, who claimed to have donated money to the Conservative Party hoping to influence Government policy in the Middle East.

Hashemi claims to have made three donations, totalling £85,000, and further alleges these donations enabled him to meet Margaret Thatcher, the former Prime Minister, to discuss easing sanctions against Iran during the period following the introduction of restrictions on the sale of defence equipment to Iran. "My purpose was to gain access to the highest level of government and try to sway it to have a better understanding of the government at war in Iran...," Hashemi is reported to have said. "I wouldn't say I was able to influence it one hundred per cent, but I let both sides say what they wanted to say about each other and to enable them to pass messages back and forth."

Following President Clinton's re-election in November 1996, a letter to the President from Mochtar Riady, the Indonesian billionaire and head of Lippo Group, demonstrating an apparent intention to influence US foreign policy in Asia was published by The Wall Street Journal. The letter was written in March 1993, following Clinton's first presidential election win, and called upon the president to normalise relations with Vietnam and to ignore human rights violations in China and Indonesia. Riady's letter also urged Clinton to increase the number of trade delegations to Asia, to appoint ambassadors with a business background to countries in the region and to grant Indonesia observer status at a summit of the Group of Seven industrial nations in Tokyo.

The activities of John Huang, the former Lippo employee, have been referred to previously and helped to initiate investigations into the propriety of Democratic Party fund-raising during the 1996 election campaign, particularly in relation to the laundering of illegal foreign contributions. Subsequent investigations by officials and the media led to further damaging revelations. In June 1996 a Thai-American businesswoman, Pauline Kanchanalak, took officials from a Thai business conglomerate, CP Group Limited, which has interests in China, to meet President Clinton. According to reports, the main topic during the meeting was US policy towards China.

On the same day, Kanchanalak and her sister-in-law contributed $135,000 to the Democratic National Committee. This donation was in addition to other donations made by Kanchanalak on other dates; $250,000 was returned to Kanchanalak after she admitted the money had been donated by her mother-in-law, as election laws forbid donations made in another's name. Several weeks later, Kanchanalak's name came once again to the fore, with reports that one of the President's personal appointees to the Export/Import Bank of the United States, Maria Haley, had allegedly pushed for the US government to help a Thai company to finance a video store franchise in Bangkok. Haley's support for the project was at variance with the view taken by others in Washington, who felt the deal fell outside the remit of the bank, which aims to encourage exports to support American employment. Amid questions about the operation of the franchise the deal did not proceed, and it was then revealed the financial package surrounding the proposed deal had been assembled, for the most part, by Pauline Kanchanalak.

Further allegations came with reports a donor to both US political parties, Occidental Petroleum Corporation, had secured an exemption to the US 1996 Anti-Terrorism Act which bans financial transactions between US companies and nations accused of fostering terrorist acts. Though Sudan appeared on the State Department list of countries as a sponsor of terrorism, the Clinton administration exempted Sudan, where Occidental was chasing an oil deal worth nearly $1 billion. The deal did not proceed.

Such is the concern about allegations of improper fund-raising that in February 1997 Federal Marshals served 44 subpoenas involving 148 people. The subpoenas were served across four continents and ordered witnesses to appear before the United States Senate as part of the inquiry into political fund raising. Observers believed evidence was being sought that US policy towards China, Taiwan, Indonesia, Thailand and even Paraguay had been influenced.

Interest in the Paraguayan connection arose with allegations that a Clinton donor, Mark Jimenez, of Future Tech International, had given $100,000 to the Democratic National Committee on the day a coup was mounted in Paraguay - the same day he was in the White House appealing to national security staff to intervene in Paraguay. President Clinton publicly opposed the coup, promising support to the Paraguayan government. The inquiry into US political fund-raising and its effects upon policy continues.

Whether influence is brought to bear upon a head of state, national government, tax inspector or minor official the problem is the same. Where there is a financial advantage to be gained, transactions must be capable of public scrutiny. Corruption will take place in the absence of light, for that is the nature of the beast. However, almost as damaging to public confidence is the belief a deal has been cut where it has not. The fact that dealings have not been open to public scrutiny taint what may be a perfectly acceptable transaction carried out in the public interest, for the dark breeds conspiracy theories as much as it breeds corruption.

In India, political corruption has reached the most senior levels. Seven leading politicians were charged recently by police. The police also sought permission to prosecute three cabinet ministers in January 1996 for allegedly receiving bribes from a prominent industrialist, Surendra Jain. After being jailed in 1994, Jain admitted he bribed politicians in return for the award of contracts and in particular, power contracts. Payments were recorded in a coded notebook with payments totalling $33 million for the years 1988 and 1992. Recipients of bribes were referred to in the notebook by their initials.

Indian police also raided the home of Sukh Ram, a former communications minister, in August 1996, and found over $1 million worth of rupees stuffed into suitcases and plastic bags. Ram supervised the process for the award of over $25 billion worth of telecommunications licences in 1995, amid opposition claims he had accepted kickbacks. The claims were referred to the Indian Supreme Court which upheld the tendering process used.

In France 14 men and women, including four civil servants, two architects and representatives of computer companies were charged with fraud and corruption offences in March 1996 in the Seine-Maritime area. It was alleged that normal procedures for the award of public contracts had been distorted to benefit favoured suppliers in return for favours. Rules for the invitation of tenders were alleged to have been broken and over-billing and the use of fake bills was suspected. Losses were estimated to be in the region of 50 million francs.

In Cannes in July 1996 Michael Mouillot, Mayor of southern French city, and Jean de Mendriguren, his Chief of Staff, were taken into custody on suspicion of attempting to extract money from the British gambling firm, London Clubs, in return for permission to install 'one armed bandits' at a casino it operates at the Carlton Hotel in Cannes. A middle man had already been arrested by Scotland Yard officers as he received three million francs (385,000) in cash at the Ritz Hotel in London.

Russian investigators recently smashed a huge racket involving illegally obtained British passports. During a drugs raid in Moscow in December 1996 , the KGB discovered about 200 UK passports which they believed were part of a supply being used by organised criminals and illegal Chinese immigrants fleeing Hong Kong before the handover. While some believe the passports were stolen from embassies, it is more likely corrupt officials were involved.

Russian gangsters are known to be heavily involved in the country's gambling industry, and in August 1996 Yuri Luzhkov, the Mayor of Moscow, ordered that the number of casinos in the city be reduced from 72 to five. Cynical observers in the city expected bureaucrats to welcome the new legislation as an opportunity to inflate the value of bribes required to secure a casino licence. As most casinos operated under protection from one of the many armed groups in Moscow, a rise in violence was anticipated as gangs vied for business in a shrinking market. Many of the gangs contain corrupt police officers keen to protect their own financial interests.

Hungarian officials launched a corruption inquiry in September 1994 into the privatisation of state companies under the previous conservative regime. It was alleged that only $722 million of the projected $1.1 billion from privatisations in 1993 had been collected. Allegations of misconduct included under valuation of companies and sales to preferred purchasers.

Chapter Nine

ARMS

"A place called in the Hebrew tongue, Armageddon"
Revelation of St John (16:16)

Every year nations spend $500 billion to meet their military needs. With so much money sloshing around there are huge rewards for those who make it into the supply chain. The arms trade is one of the few areas of business where good salesmen can create a 'snowball effect' for sales. By playing off nation against nation, political faction against political faction and heightening almost primeval feelings of insecurity, sales are increased.

In this age of high technology, the costs of research and development in the arms industry are immense. The cost of development, the tooling-up of production lines and weapon-proving cannot be met, for the most part, from a domestic peace time market. The dilemma is that nobody can say with any certainty when production for the domestic market might need to be rapidly increased to meet some international crisis or conflict. National governments therefore want to place defence orders to meet minimum defence requirements, but keep production lines open to permit future flexibility should the need arise.

Apart from the entrepreneurial spirit which propels all manufacturers and salespeople, whatever their product, the need to recoup massive research and development costs and to keep production lines open are the impetus for foreign arms sales. As a result there is a certain amount of cynicism, some would say pragmatism, exhibited within the great arms exporting nations such as Britain and France.

As already discussed, Lord Young, Chairman of Cable and Wireless, takes this tack and a similar view was voiced by the Labour MP John Stonehouse, a vociferous supporter of arms sales in Harold Wilson's 1964 government. Following a trip to Saudi Arabia, Stonehouse, speaking about commissions and intermediaries in the arms trade, wrote: "What was the point of adopting a 'holier than thou' attitude when Britain's factories sorely needed the business...".

There is also an opinion that if the value of a contract is inflated to allow for 'grease' payments and commissions, it should not trouble the suppliers as it is not their money being used, but that of the purchaser nation. It is another example of expedience, but it side-steps the point that many arms deals are funded, perhaps indirectly, by aid from the supplier nation and their tax-payers.

ARMS producing nations often exploit other countries to support their indigenous arms industries, placing a burden on their treasuries at the expense of more pressing areas such as health, welfare and education. Improper practices used by many in the arms trade can distort whole national economies.

As in so many other areas which are examined in this book, it may be difficult to know where to draw the line between sharp and improper practice in the quest for arms sales. In 1988 the British Defence Secretary George Younger visited Malaysia to foster UK arms sales. Younger was seeking a massive £1 billion arms deal; the Malaysians were seeking foreign aid in the region of £420 million to build a dam. But arms deals as a quid pro quo for aid packages are barred; thus began the Pergau Dam affair.

It transpired two letters had been sent to Kuala Lumpur from London on the same day; one confirming the arms deal, the other offering the required assistance to fund the Pergau project. It was to be financed in part with money from the British Governments Aid and Trade fund, known in Whitehall as the 'slush fund' but it was another three years before the deal hit the headlines.

The UK Overseas Development Administration raised objections on the grounds of cost, the effects on the surrounding environment and efficacy. The matter came to a head in the winter of 1993/94 when The Sunday Times newspaper published a story linking the aid with the supply of arms. The reports in the paper attracted the ire of the Malaysian Government, which threatened to break all trade links with the United Kingdom if the UK press could not be kept under control.

Amid growing pressure on the Conservative government, the House of Commons Committee on Foreign Affairs was asked to investigate. The committee's report, delivered in July 1994, criticised the government's handling of the affair and the action taken by ministers once the affair had attracted attention: "Ministerial replies were literally true, though less open and informative than the House has a right to expect." The report also stated: "We consider it reprehensible for the Ministry of Defence to have prepared for, and conducted, negotiations with another country in 1988, without specific reference to the Foreign and Commonwealth Office as soon as it was known that the other party wished to add to those talks a dimension falling within the FCO's remit." In addition, the committee was "...particularly concerned that this should have occurred in relation to such a sensitive issue as a conditional linkage between development aid and defence sales, which was contrary to stated government policy."

In the USA, there are strict laws preventing the offering of inducements to win foreign contracts. The Arms Export Control Act prohibits the payment of commissions on arms deals. There are, however, ingenious methods which may be employed by US arms suppliers to circumvent its provisions. In 1995 Senator Russ Feingold of Wisconsin protested that a Wisconsin paper company had suffered an unfair disadvantage because the US Northrop Corporation was offering a $1 million discount to another US paper company to persuade it to import paper from a paper processing plant in Finland. Northrop wanted to generate $2 billion worth of Finnish imports to the United States. In return, the Finnish government would order $3 billion worth of fighter aircraft from Northrop.

BOTH the Pergau Dam affair and the Northrop example demonstrate the lengths to which Western nations will go to promote arms sales without resorting to actual bribery, but what of the distortions to economies?

In his seminal work on the arms trade, 'The Arms Bazaar', Anthony Sampson cites the example of the Lockheed Corporations most profitable export of the 1960's: the Hercules C130 military transport aircraft which played a huge role in the economy of the US state of Georgia where it was produced. When asked by Sampson as to why Lockheed needed to market the aircraft so aggressively when the company had a virtual monopoly, an executive replied, "We're always competing with other government projects". The selling of the Hercules to other states was also acknowledged to be of special interest to the Pentagon, as it wished to keep the production line in Georgia open in case the Pentagon should require more planes for US defence purposes.

Sampson provides an example of the effect of Lockheed's almost evangelical style of salesmanship in Colombia in 1972, when a reduction in the Colombian military budget had been requested by the country's President. Lockheed's man on the ground in Bogota learned that 'high officers of the air force' would arrange for further purchases in return for bribes in the sum of $100,000, thereby ignoring the call for a reduction in the military budget. As Anthony Sampson puts it, "The meaning was unambiguous: the point of the bribe was to sell arms, where arms were not needed."

Sampson also quotes from research on Indonesian defence spending, as investigated in 'The Arms Trade and The Third World', a Stockholm International Peace Research Institute report of 1971. Under President Sukarno in the 1960's, the report stated, Indonesia was spending 75% of its national budget on arms. The report referred to Indonesia, a haven for arms salesmen, as "an underdeveloped country preoccupied with a military build-up that is out of proportion to its economic resources."

But what of the wealthier nations - like Saudi Arabia, an oil rich country with a military build-up out of all proportion to its defence needs? Despite huge spending on defence since the 1970's, Saudi Arabia on its own was unable to face the threat from Iraq during the Gulf crisis of 1990. This situation was not the result of a lack of spending upon arms, but rather a realisation that the purchase of high technology war materials could not alone produce an effective military deterrent.

The simple truth is that Saudi Arabia has more arms than its defence forces can use and is reliant upon the West for its protection. An overt reliance on the West, however, does not attract favour from other Arab nations, nor the strong Muslim fundamentalist movement within the country, and this is a factor behind the sham defence policy promulgated by the country's rulers. The huge arms procurement process founded upon this pretence has proven to be fertile ground for high-powered middlemen who secure billions of dollars in 'commissions' by selling influence drawn from their close relationships with members of the House of Saud.

The result of this naive defence policy and the frenetic activity of arms suppliers and intermediaries has been to direct funds needed to develop a country, with only 55% literacy, towards wasteful arms procurement and produce economic distortions which may prove disastrous for the regime.

Under the Shah's 'Peacock Throne' in Iran there were plenty of examples where threatening religious fervour was used to justify a defence policy which demanded more arms than Iran actually needed, a demand fuelled by the payment of commissions. Money spent on arms is money wasted at the cost of development, a lesson the Shah learnt the hard way during the revolution.

According to Said K Aburish in his excellent book, 'The Rise, Corruption and Coming fall of the House of Saud', between 1979 and 1994 Saudi Arabia's arms procurement budget averaged between $12 billion and $18 billion per year to supply armed forces numbering in the region of 110,000. The procurement figures do not make logistical sense when compared to the number of personnel.

Aburish cites examples such as the Saudi Air Academy, built in 1984 to accommodate 50,000 cadets, instructors and other staff. It has never held more than 6,000 occupants and with an air force strength of 15,000 is never likely to. Then there is the Hafr Al Batin army base, built to house 14,000 staff and home to only 2,000; 15 airforce bases in Qutaif are chronically undermanned, one has only three staff. He also lists tanks, howitzers, naval vessels and aircraft and compares them to the number of available staff. The result is always the same: too many weapons systems, too few troops.

So why are they overspending? Perhaps the building of a strong defence force, independent of Western protection, is a pretext and the Saudis are actually stockpiling weapons for use by Western forces in case of emergency. At first glance, this theory seems credible. NATO defence policy in Western Europe during the Cold War included similar stockpiling of heavy weaponry for use by US troops. The theory disintegrates however when one considers the diversity of the equipment purchased by the Saudis: Chinese ground-to-ground missiles, American, French and British armoured vehicles, American and British aircraft. No attempt has been made to co-ordinate purchases.

The pursuit of Western commercial interest and the desire for commissions by middle men has led to a totally unbalanced defence procurement policy and an unbalanced Saudi Arabian economy. The Saudis spend 30% of their annual budget on arms and have been deluded into thinking they are necessary.

THE LESS democratic countries of Africa, Asia, South America and the Middle East may be prey to bribery and corruption but the developed countries of the West could be just as bad but better at covering their tracks. In the 1970's, a Senate Sub-committee on Multinational Corporations, chaired by Senator Frank Church, discovered that public officials in Japan, the Netherlands and Italy, had been bought by American firms as easily as any third world potentate.

The American aircraft corporations, led in their efforts by Lockheed and Northrop, paid millions of dollars in bribes to senior figures officials. Lockheed operated a corporate code book, revised periodically, in which Giovanni Leone, the Italian Prime Minister was identified under the code name 'Antelope Cobbler'. In an edition dated 15th October 1965 'Antelope' stood for Italy, 'Cobbler' for premier. Antelope Cobbler's role was to ensure the Italian Air Force bought Lockheed C130 Hercules transport planes at a cost of $4 million each.

The reward for Cobbler? $120,000 was paid for every aircraft purchased, money which Leone's Christian Democratic Party badly needed. Fourteen aircraft were bought and payments in support of the deal came to about $2 million, with $1.7 million shown in Lockheed documents as 'promotional expenses'. The same document noted that 85% of the $1.7 million was for Leone's political party. It was said Italy did not need 14 long-range cargo planes. The Americans just shrugged their shoulders: the order certainly kept the Lockheed production line in Georgia busy.

The evidence laid before the Church Committee also indicated Lockheed had paid $12 million to Japanese officials, including the former Japanese premier, Kakuei Tanaka. Tanaka was arrested in 1976 and charged with accepting $1.2 million in bribes from Lockheed for arranging for the Japanese navy to order Orion anti-submarine aircraft and for the purchase by Japanese Airlines of Lockheed TriStars. In common with Leone, Tanaka was accused of taking money for political purposes.

Prince Bernhard of the Netherlands, however, did not want money to play in the great game of politics. He solicited bribes for himself through his position in the Dutch military establishment and in the government, vantage points from where he was able to influence aircraft procurement. Lockheed admitted to the Church Committee that $1 million in bribes had been paid to 'a high Dutch official'. Leaks led the press to suspect the official was no less than Prince Bernhard, husband of Queen Julianna. As a result, the Dutch Prime Minister appointed a committee of investigation. With the later revelation of two letters to Lockheed demanding money, the Prince was forced to resign all his public positions.

WERE these instances mere 'blips' in an otherwise competitive but scrupulous industry? Not at all, as we can still see from more recent examples. The down-sizing in the European defence industry has led to a drop in employment of more than 50% over the period 1986-1996 and has envenomed the market place.

In Belgium the Agusta helicopters affair surfaced as a result of the assassination of a politician in front of his young mistress's home on a summer morning in July 1991. The dead politician, Andre Cools, the 63-year-old former Deputy Prime Minister, former president of the Socialist Party and mayor of the town of Flemalle, was shot in the car park of a block of flats in a prosperous area on the outskirts of Liege. His mistress, with whom he had spent the night, was seriously wounded.

The incident led to an investigation headed by an examining magistrate, Veronique Ancia, which has revealed high-level corruption and led to resignations and even suicide. During the course of the investigation, Ancia took evidence from a leading Belgian socialist, Alain Vanderbiest, who had taken over from the assassinated Cools in the party hierarchy. While denying any involvement in the murder, Vanderbiest admitted to occasional irregularities in the financing of the Belgian Socialist Party.

While accepting Vanderbiest's denial of implication in the murder, his references to Party financing led Ancia to conduct a search of the Party's Liege offices. It revealed details of Swiss bank accounts and unexplained references to the Italian helicopter company, Agusta. Further searches at Agusta's Belgian subsidiary uncovered further documents referring to 'commissions' to be paid in relation to a deal for the purchase of 46 Agusta helicopters by the Belgian army for a sum in the region of £600 million. The murder enquiry took on a completely different complexion.

In 1983 the Belgian army had decided its helicopter fleet needed updating. A decision upon replacement aircraft was not made until 1988, and almost up to the very point when the deal was signed, experts had recommended French or German equipment with Agusta A109 helicopters coming a poor third. Against all the odds Agusta won the contest on the basis of what were described as 'compensation payments'. In a formula proposed by Agusta, part of the purchase price of the helicopters would be returned to the Liege region as investment in the form of factories making spare parts. And as the local party head, André Cools had approached the then Belgian Prime Minister, Willy Claes, later NATO Secretary General, to secure support for the proposed deal.

As previously reported, the ensuing investigations into the financing of the Belgian Socialist Party led to the resignation of a number of Belgian officials and the resignation of Willy Claes as Secretary General of NATO. A separate investigation in Italy headed by the 'Clean Hands' anti-corruption team led in April 1993 to the arrest of the President of Agusta, Roberto d'Alessandro, on charges of bribery related to the sale of helicopters to the Italian security forces.

Allegations were also levelled at the former chief of the Belgian air force, Jacques Lefèbvre, in a Belgian television programme in March 1995, which was followed by his suicide immediately afterwards. Further enquiries into the activities of Lefèbvre have turned attention towards French aircraft manufacturers, notably Dassault.

In May 1996, an international arrest warrant was issued by the Belgian judiciary to force Serge Dassault, the head of the French aircraft manufacturer of the same name, to answer bribery allegations in relation to the supply of electronic defence systems to the Belgian air force in 1989. Dassault voiced his intention to remain in France, apparently relying upon a French policy of not extraditing French nationals.

The Belgian authorities alleged bribes totalling $2.88 million had been paid to secure business worth $210 million. It is alleged most of the money was paid to the Flemish Socialist Party, although approximately $900,000 remains unaccounted for. Despite the repercussions for Belgian politics and French and Italian aircraft manufacturers, the Cools murder case remains unsolved.

At the same time that Belgian investigators were probing the arcane methods of military aircraft procurement and political party funding across Europe, Britain had its own arms procurement scandal. In May 1994, Bernard Trevelyan, former head of the Ministry of Defence's Light Armoured Engineering Systems Department, was jailed for one year following a trial at Southwark Crown Court on four charges of corruption. Trevelyan had, in his official capacity, great influence in the awarding of

Cartoon by Sidney Harris

"Mr. Cummings will now discuss that gray area between legal acts and illegal acts."

Global Ethics, Spring 1995

A wry commentary on the fine line between normal business dealings and corruption.

contracts for armoured car equipment. Using a front company, Surrey Consultants, he disguised illicit payments he received in return for leaking technical and financial information and influencing the award of contracts.

But Trevelyan's gains of nearly £10,000 were minuscule in comparison with those made by Gordon Foxley, a former director of the Ministry of Defences Munitions Procurement Department, who was sentenced to four years imprisonment on 26th May 1994, again on corruption charges. Foxley was paid £1.3 million in bribes by foreign arms companies in a scheme of corruption which lasted between 1979 and 1994, when he retired from the MoD. Though Foxley had never earned more than £25,000 per year as a civil servant, he lived in a mansion at Henley on Thames, valued in excess of £500,000, and purchased luxury properties and a fleet of luxury cars.

The firms bribing Foxley for the award of contracts were based in Germany, Norway and Italy. It contradicts the notion that there is a supposed 'gentleman's agreement' which some imagine to exist between the developed nations, precluding the payment of bribes.

In October 1994 details of the financial damage estimated to have been caused by Foxley's actions were calculated by accountants. The costs included redundancy and unemployment benefits for workers who lost their jobs at the Royal Ordinance Factory (which lost contracts to firms bribing Foxley) in Lancashire, worker retraining costs and the decline in the sale price of the firm when it was privatised due to lost contracts.

When the cost of purchasing supplies from the foreign companies bribing Foxley was added to all the foregoing calculations, it was estimated The cost to the British taxpayer was £15 million, according to experts.

What of the moral standards of those nations bribing Foxley and Belgian officials? We in the United Kingdom feel outraged that public officials would take bribes to advance the interests of other nations to the detriment of the home economy. Yet those carrying out the bribery to win the business would probably argue that there is no moral problem, it is simply a matter of jobs, and decry adopting a 'holier than thou attitude'. 'What goes around, comes around' is a useful maxim in the world of arms dealing.

The benefits of commercial corruption can be vast: secret bank records were finally handed over to **India** in 1997 which contained the names of politicians who took bribes from the Swedish arms manufacturer Bofors in the 1980s. India purchased 410 field guns from Bofors for £1.3 billion and allegations of corruption were made in the Indian press. The following month, Indian investigators proposed extradition proceedings against an Italian businessman, Ottavio Quattrocchi, who had been part of the inner circle of the late Indian prime minister, Rajiv Gandhi.

The **Swedish** arms manufacturer, Kockums, allegedly contributed funds to the campaign war chest of Thai politicians during the July 1995 parliamentary elections in the hope of winning a contract to supply two submarines worth £680 million to the Thai navy. It is illegal for Thai politicians to accept contributions from foreign companies. In an editorial on the controversy, one Thai newspaper stated, "...the general feeling is that there are opportunities for politicians to make money if they can get to the top and be in the right place at the right time, and this disgusts many."

In October 1994 an international arbitration court agreed, in principle, with an **Iranian** government claim for the return of a down payment of $150 million to German ship building company, Howaldtswerke Deutsche Werft AF (HDW), made in 1978. The money was intended as the initial payment for six submarines with a total value of $650 million. Iran paid advanced $650 million, whereupon over $70 million was transferred by HDW to a numbered Swiss account under the control of Shah Reza Pahlevi. The vessels were never delivered and as a result, Iran reclaimed the monies paid. HDW, at the relevant time a state owned company, argued its liability should be covered by the German taxpayer.

In January 1996 the national security adviser of former **South Korean** President Roh Tae Woo acknowledged he had received money from businesses hoping to win arms contracts from the South Korean government totalling nearly $300,000.

Chapter Ten

ORGANISED CRIME

"May you live in turbulent times"
Chinese curse

SINCE the first police forces were established, there have been continual allegations of police corruption. London's Metropolitan Police was founded in 1829, a time of graft and violence on the streets of the city, and the quality of the first recruits left much to be desired. Within the first two years 1,989 officers had been dismissed, mainly for drunkenness but opportunities for abuse of office and petty corruption were rife.

Over the succeeding decades, complaints continued with sporadic attempts to clean up the various forces. However, the 1970s brought a series of police-corruption show-trials in London with criticism levelled at the robbery, drugs and pornography squads.

Operation Countryman was established as a result of allegations of corrupt relationships between professional criminals and officers in the City of London police (who cover London's financial area containing the Stock Exchange and the Bank of England). The enquiry was later extended to investigations within the Metropolitan Police without great success if one measures the number of prosecutions and convictions. Most of the allegations levelled in the 1970s involved payment to police officers from petty thieves and burglars seeking bail. Criminals from the higher echelons, such as bank robbers and pornographers, wanted protection from prosecution.

British criminal gangs certainly existed but were generally loose associations based upon family or geographical location. Organised crime's effect upon broader society was limited, largely by a lack of funds. This contrasted with the United States where prohibition had provided the oxygen required to create an inferno of crime.

The temperance movement, with its avowed intentions of saving the populace from the demon drink, actually did no more than leave a vacuum of supply which was filled by criminal enterprise. It handed those with criminal aspirations an extremely lucrative industry, and the wealth generated by this industry allowed organised crime to dig in to society - corrupting, draining and distorting as it progressed.

If prohibition provided the catalyst for the intrusion of organised crime into the wider economic and political world in the United States, then an even greater danger is the great wealth generated by the world trade in illicit drugs and the allegiances being forged by criminal gangs across the globe. Estimates put the value of the world drug trade at $500 billion per year. The gangs know that protecting this trade is worth ensuring law enforcement officials, judges and politicians are 'taken care of'.

The potential for corruption arising from crime has therefore gone far beyond bribes for bail or the turning of a blind eye to allow robbers to escape justice. Organised crime is a cancer pervading established democratic states and choking off the efforts of those seeking to develop. As London underworld gangs or New York Mafia families once laid claim to areas of influence within their respective cities, so major international crime syndicates are now carving out spheres of influence for themselves throughout the world.

The sums of money at their disposal surpass the gross domestic product of many third world nations and rival that of some of the smaller developed nations. There is also strong evidence that criminal organisations have formal alliances and 'treaties'. The bonds between the Sicilian and American Mafias, the Russian Mafia, Chinese Triads and Japanese Yakuza gangsters have left the world open to exploitation and plunder.

THE REBEL armies of Burma, Laos and Thailand are the world's chief heroin producers and the illegal trade in this 'Golden Triangle' is dominated by Burma, which is now the world's leading producer of opium, the raw material for the production of heroin, with an estimated annual output of 2,600 tons. Laos is the world's third largest producer, but its weak, nominally Marxist Leninist government makes it an ideal staging and refining point for drugs on their way to the international drugs market. The tiny salaries paid to Laotian soldiers and officers make high levels of corruption almost inevitable among those who are supposed to stop the trade.

"The role of drugs in Burma's economic and political life and the regime's refusal to honour it's own pledge to move to multi-party democracy are really two sides of the same coin," said President Clinton on a post 1996 election tour of Asia and Australia in recognition of high level corruption in the area. Clinton went on to praise the Burmese opposition: "Only true political dialogue." could lead to a "real fight against crime, corruption and narcotics."

ON THE OTHER side of the world, the Latin American countries of Colombia, Peru and Bolivia produce huge amounts of cocaine. Here too, illicit drug production and the huge profits thereby gained have tainted economies and political systems.

In August 1996 "El Vaticano" Demetrio Chavez Penaherrera, one of Peru's top drug traffickers in the early 1990s, testified before a court trying him for drug trafficking, that in 1991-2 he had been paying $50,000 per month to a top intelligence adviser, Vladimiro Montesinos, to protect his drugs flights into Columbia. These claims were later retracted and a former general was imprisoned on drugs charges arising out of the same matter. General Jaime Rios was jailed for 15 years for aiding Penaherrera, who was given 25 years. Rios was accused of taking payment for drug airlifts and of accepting supplies from those involved in drug trafficking. However this was only the latest in a series of drugs related incidents which have embarrassed the Peruvian government. In one incident, 174 kilos of coca paste were found in a former presidential plane, soon to be followed by the discovery of 100 kilos on board two navy ships, one in port in Vancouver, Canada.

In Venezuela the police are officially in charge of investigating drugs offences. However decrees aimed at controlling the activities of Shining Path guerrillas have given the military control of some of the major drug trafficking areas. 'El Vaticano's' airstrip was only a few kilometres from a counter-insurgency base in the Hualanga Valley, and the drug baron was known to be bribing a number of the officers. Approximately 300 members of the armed forces in Peru have been investigated in connection with drugs offences since 1990, in a country with an estimated 930 square miles of coca under cultivation, accounting for 60% of the world supply.

Allegations have also been made against those in public life in Columbia, another cocaine producing country, with a well-deserved reputation for violence and sleaze. This reputation is based on its expertise in refining and distributing cocaine, as the country actually accounts for only 10% of world cocaine production. The sleaze reaches the highest levels: President Samper faced a major political crisis stemming from allegations that his 1994 election campaign fund was swelled by some $6 million donated by the Cali cocaine cartel. The President insisted he was unaware of such donations and he was twice cleared of any impropriety by the Colombian Congress.

Close aides of President Samper have however been jailed for illegally enriching themselves with drug traffickers money. There was further controversy when 7lb of heroin was found on board the Presidential Boeing 707 aircraft a few hours before it was due to convey the president to New York to address the United Nations on a global anti drugs strategy. The President called the incident 'a nasty conspiracy' aimed at discrediting him. Other ministers hinted at an 'international plot' to force President Samper's downfall.

This belief that drug traffickers are subverting some political administrations is a view held within the US State Department. In September 1996 Jane Becker, an assistant secretary of state said, "Traffickers have penetrated the highest levels of society and government institutions in Antigua, Barbuda, Trinidad and Tobago, St Kitts and Nevis, Aruba, Jamaica and the Dominican Republic."

Her statement followed an FBI and Justice Department investigation into money laundering where the main targets identified were Caribbean islands with offshore banking facilities used to launder huge sums of money and whose institutions were as a result, subverted to the will of the traffickers.

HAVING established the sources of these drugs, it should be asked which criminal organisations are seeking to exploit the availability of such merchandise and what makes them such a threat. As already stated, the main criminal organisations are the Italian/American Mafias, Russian Mafias, Chinese Triads and Japanese Yakuza. That these groups pose such a threat lies in their organisation; they share a common thread which lies in history. Their strength derives from structures formed in the face of past opposition, structures which have left these organisations perfectly poised to exploit lucrative criminal opportunities.

In 1860 Guiseppe Garibaldi overthrew Bourbon rule in Sicily, his small army augmented by groups of bandits. Subjected to foreign rule, Sicilians had learned to despise authority - which they equated with foreign oppression. The bands they formed by way of resistance had similar codes of honour: help for the poor against the rich, mutual aid between members, obedience to the chief, offence against one was offence to all and the secrets of the group were never to be disclosed to those outside. A cell structure among the groups lent itself to security by ensuring no one member could know the full extent of the group's activities. These were the origins of the Mafia in Sicily, though there were other areas in Italy where secret societies existed, notably Naples, which was also under Bourbon rule until 1860. The secret society there was called the Camorra, which enforced similar rules to those of the Sicilian Mafia upon its members. The populist appeal of these organisations (working for the people in the face of foreign oppression) soon gave way to crime for profit.

Other political activists who used criminals to fight against the established order were the Bolsheviks in Tsarist Russia, who harnessed the rebellious talents of criminals to spread public disorder through assassinations, robbery and large scale theft.

Having used the criminals towards their own ends, the communists later cracked down hard upon them. But not quite hard enough to wipe them out or the underground organisation which they had formed with a code of ethics and behaviour. Following Stalin, this criminal underground went from strength to strength as it allied itself to the political elite, and set about furthering its own ends itself by bleeding the state through large scale theft and corruption.

CHINESE Triad societies find their origins in patriotic organisations which existed in the face of opposition from the foreign Ch'ing dynasty, which was imposed by Manchu invaders in 1644 after the ruling Ming dynasty had been deposed. Rules of secrecy, honour and obedience were instilled into new members along with a hierarchy of roles: 'Straw sandal' for the initiate who might advance to 'Red Pole' (a fighter), 'White Paper Fan' (accountant) or eventually to 'Hill Chief'. In contrast, the secret ways of the Japanese Yakuza are protected not only through oaths of loyalty, but by reliance upon Japanese culture and the fear of losing face. This fear has allowed the Yakuza to blackmail large companies who will pay large sums rather than have stockholders meetings disrupted by gangsters holding a few company shares, which provide a ticket into the meeting. Similarly, the victims of Yakuza loan sharking operations suffer in silence or, when the burden becomes too great, commit suicide rather than denounce their persecutors and risk acknowledging human frailty.

The very existence of Japanese organised crime was not recognised by Japanese government, again seeking to maintain face, until the Yakuza were outlawed in January 1992. Romantics say the Yakuza came into being in the seventeenth century as a response from young men of honour in resistance to the excesses of Samurai Warriors. A more plausible version roots the Yakuza in the tightly-disciplined Bakuto gangs who travelled eighteenth century Japan gambling and using the word 'Yakusa' for a worthless hand of cards.

ALL THESE crime groups can all claim a history and all have cell-like structures formed as a result of the environment from which they evolved. These structures make them more difficult to penetrate by those outside the grouping. Their tight organisation gives them a decided advantage when exploiting the opportunities from the trade in illicit goods and services, mainly the trafficking of drugs.

The disintegration of the Soviet bloc with the resultant break down of the administrative machinery of its member states has created a further threat. Since the disintegration, the economies of Eastern European states and the former Soviet Union have been plundered by organised crime syndicates. These usually act in concert to subvert authority, secure freedom of movement without intervention and to empty the national coffers and drain the natural resources. In turn the syndicates from the West and the Far East have wasted no time in using the 'Klondike' atmosphere of the former Soviet Union to 'invest' and launder their criminal gains made elsewhere in the world.

Some observers believe that the Italian and American Mafia are in decline due to the increasing successes scored by law enforcement agencies in both countries. Forty two Mafia bosses were convicted in the USA during the three year period ending in December 1996. In December 1996 38 Mafia members were sentenced to a total of 328 years imprisonment by a court in Sicily, marking the end of an investigation set in train by the two murdered anti-Mafia judges, Giovanni Falcone and Paolo Borsellino, who were blown up within a month of each other in Sicily in 1992.

The arrest of Salvatore 'Toto' Riina, the Cosa Nostra's supreme godfather in January 1993 was seen by some analysts as shadowing the upheaval in Italy caused by the 'Clean Hands' investigations into political corruption with the undermining of senior politicians by scandals. There was a view that the post-war generation which had kept a stranglehold on power, both through corruption and organised crime, was being challenged, with criminals no longer able to rely upon corrupt Italian politicians and judges to help them when in need.

This is not a view subscribed to by one of Palermo's most experienced prosecutors, Vittorio Teresi, who quotes the example of the town of Agrigento: There "the award of public contracts is still entirely controlled by Cosa Nostra and its political and economic contacts. In Palermo, there is not a single supermarket which is not directly or indirectly controlled by its clans. The Mafia has always had an inverse capacity for rehabilitation and after its traditional political godfathers fell, it soon found others."

Faced with the assault from law enforcement agencies in Italy and the USA, the Mafia has therefore been forced to move into new areas and new alliances, most notably with organised crime groups in Russia, an analysis supported by Major General Verdicchio, a senior officer of the Italian financial police, who speaking at a meeting in London in June, 1996 said: "The Italian Mafia is laundering money out of the former Soviet Union to rebuild itself financially because of the clampdown on its operations domestically."

Umberto Santino, a Palermo sociologist, believes the Italian Mafia has been moving in recent times out of drug trafficking and into fraud, involving European Union funds and 'investment' in Eastern Europe. This investment, however, is not intended to benefit the recipient country, only the organised crime syndicates involved and corrupt public officials who ease their way.

In recognition of the threat posed to Russia by organised crime President Yeltsin called the Mafia his 'country's greatest single problem' in

February 1993. The effect of such rampant crime and official collusion is also well illustrated by comments made by the then British Foreign Secretary, Douglas Hurd, at a G7 meeting the following month when he advised against investment in Russia. He referred to the Russian economy as 'a pocket with holes in it'.

The rape of Russia by organised crime has had three effects: many Russian officials have been corrupted by the huge amounts of money utilised by organised crime to dominate the system. Those that are not corrupted face assassination. Secondly, the subversion of the guardians of the state, both politicians and law enforcement officers, has allowed a feeding frenzy of predators to take place, stripping the natural resources and economy. Thirdly, the huge profits made by organised crime and withdrawn from Russia have strengthened the efforts of those criminal syndicates to infiltrate other national systems to make further financial gains and to obtain protection for their gains.

As the USA became the champion of democracy in the 1940s, Russia has alas become the force behind organised crime's assault upon the Western world. Russia is the largest laundry for illicit money and many cash-starved military forces are now so corrupt that sophisticated weapons are sold openly to criminal syndicates.

The most striking example of the acquisition, or in this case attempted acquisition, of high technology weaponry by organised crime elements come with the allegation in February 1997 that American government surveillance had uncovered a plot to sell a Russian nuclear powered Piranha class attack submarine to Colombian drug barons for use in smuggling. The man accused over the submarine sale, along with two associates, was Ludwig Fainberg, a Miami strip club owner, who allegedly negotiated on behalf of South American cocaine suppliers, for the purchase of 'submarines, helicopters and airplanes from the former Soviet Union', to quote the indictment before the court.

While it was unclear how the Russian authorities were going to be persuaded to allow the removal of the submarine from the Kronstadt naval base, Frank Ciluffo of the Centre for Strategic and International Studies in Washington, voiced the widely held view of experts that in the former USSR, "almost anything is for sale at a price". In addition to the diversion of hardware, Ciluffo stated, "you also have systemic corruption with a number of officials moonlighting."

IT HAS been said the Italian Mafia was a state within a state, but that imagery has now been surpassed, with criminal organisations that have the economic clout of nation states. In common with nation states, they have their allies, their enemies, their armed forces, and their intelligence services. Where they hold great advantage over nation states is in not respecting national borders; they are supranational, where borders and laws create hurdles for those who seek to curtail their operations. The crime syndicates are aggressive in their development of business opportunities and ruthless in their own defence. In furtherance of their acquisitive or defensive needs, they will not hesitate to corrupt.

THERE HAVE been a number of recent examples which illustrate how dangerous a threat crime syndicates pose in Europe. It is only recently that the threat has been taken seriously with the realisation organised criminals will seek to exploit those public officials who are supposed to stop them.

In June 1996 a police officer, Detective Constable John Donald, was jailed for 11 years on corruption charges. Donald, a former member of the South East Regional Crime Squad, tried to negotiate a £10,000 payment to pass on sensitive police information to two alleged drug runners that they were being watched. In passing sentence at the Old Bailey, Mrs Justice Steel told him: "The sentence must not only punish you but deter any other police officers who may be tempted." However, she felt that his 'greatest betrayal' had been to compromise an operation targeted on suspected importation of drugs into Britain from the United States.

A few months later a police computer expert, Nick Wheeler, was decapitated after driving his car into the back of a parked lorry, 48 hours before he was due to appear in court accused of attempting to pervert the course of justice by selling police intelligence to major criminals. Wheeler was accused after an investigation by the Kent police into why major cases were regularly collapsing. They alleged that Wheeler had been contacting criminals and offering compromising information in return for money.

In December 1996 there were further allegations that a traitor within the Customs and Excise drugs investigators in London had been supplying tip-offs to drugs barons leading to the collapse of prosecutions and drugs raids. The allegations were spiced-up by an internal mole hunt by the Security Service (MI5), an organisation which has been pushing for a

A dramatic view of the battle against corruption: the stars of a Hong Kong television series based on the work of the Independent Commission Against Corruption (ICAC) battle with gun-wielding criminals

greater role in the fight against organised crime since the collapse of the Soviet bloc and the end of the Cold War. In October 1996 MI5 was empowered to enter the fight with operations to infiltrate criminal gangs and to gather financial intelligence in attempts to track and confiscate criminal money. There is also evidence that suggests consideration is being given to allowing military forces and, in particular, elite military special forces to assist in law enforcement operations against major criminal organisations.

While considering future roles for the armed services, the British Defence Research Agency has identified the possibility that conflict between nation states may in future become less of a security threat than that posed by terrorism and organised crime.

This is a view supported by David Bickford, former legal adviser to both the Security Service (MI5) and the Secret Intelligence Service (MI6) who has identified the fact that: "many trans-national criminal organisations have a formal governing structure and are economically stronger than most UN states". He adds: "There is every reason therefore to treat criminal gangs as organisations, not as individuals."

The links between crime and politics are well-established. One of the most astonishing examples emerged during a board of enquiry set up in **Turkey** following a fatal car crash in 1996. It was quickly discovered that the only survivor, Sedat Bucak, a politician from the governing True Path Party, had been travelling in the same Mercedes as gangster Abdullah Catli and Catli's girlfriend, a former beauty queen. The situation was exacerbated by the fact that Catli had been on the run for eighteen years, wanted for the torture and murder of seven left wing students in 1978. Unlicensed weapons were also allegedly found in the car. The Turkish Interior Minister, Mehmet Agar, was forced to resign in November 1996 after his efforts to cover up the circumstances of the crash were exposed.

In **Italy** in January 1997 Giulio Andreotti, Italy's former Prime Minister, strongly denied meeting the 'godfather' of the Catania Mafia, saying that he would appeal to the European Court of Justice over his prosecution for alleged membership of Cosa Nostra. A police informer, Vito Di Maggio, told a court that in 1979, he had witnessed such a meeting. Signor Andreotti insisted Di Maggio's testimony was a total fabrication and claimed that he could prove he was abroad at the time.

Even the **USA** has been affected. In February 1997 it was disclosed that a convicted criminal with alleged links to the Mafia had enjoyed 'face time' with President Clinton as a result of contributions to the Democratic Party. Eric Wynn, a New Jersey stock promoter, was among eight guests who joined Clinton for coffee in 1995, just months after being convicted of stock manipulation. Wynn allegedly set up an account to benefit the family of a member of the Bonanno crime family.

Rio police raided offices in 1994 and found lists of politicians, policemen, journalists and celebrities allegedly in the pay of organised crime. **Brazilian** prosecutor Antonio Carlos said: "Organised crime was preparing to take over political domination of the state of Rio. They already have councillors, state and even federal deputies in their pockets." The mayor of Rio and the chief of the civil police denied involvement.

A confidential report commissioned by the European Union intended for European police forces was leaked in 1996 which revealed that **Morocco** had become the worlds largest exporter of hashish and claimed this dubious honour had been achieved by a 'very well organised hierarchical structure' involving the collusion of "civil servants customs officials and politicians through every echelon of the administration."

Chapter Eleven

THE
DAMAGE
CAUSED

"Without virtue the Republic is an empty shell and its strength becomes
merely the power of a few citizens and the licence of all."
Montesquieu

One central tenet running through this book is my belief that 'sleaze' damages democratic states and can hinder the advent of democracy. However in its most powerful forms corruption can actually supplant democracy, forming a stabilising and governing force that is almost mediaeval in character.

Lord Young has propounded the argument that money paid to the heads of certain countries will work its way through the national economy creating benefit for all - the 'trickle-down' theory. It raises the question whether the payment of bribes at one end of the scale, or the cutting of corners for friends at the other, really causes a great deal of damage. Are not some of these payments, favoured relationships and networks of contacts simply economic and political lubricants to minimise bureaucratic friction within systems, thereby causing little harm? The evidence from all around us is to the contrary.

The misuse of power and the exercise of undue influence varies in its effects according to the level of development reached in a particular country. The exercise of any undue influence distorts the decision-making process in whichever area the influence is applied, whether it be political, economic, or the enforcement of law.

Criminals are allowed to walk free, contracts are entered into which incur greater public cost, or substandard or unwanted goods are supplied. However, because the costs are dissipated throughout the whole population, the true damage is disguised and the impact diluted, especially in more developed countries.

137

In Britain, corruption was widely seen as a foreign problem until the sleaze allegations of the 1990s undermined public faith in the political system. A specially commissioned NOP poll in July 1996 revealed, among other things, that only 20% of those polled believed that British politics is less corrupt than in other countries, with 58% believing that standards in Britain were no better than anywhere else in the world. Nearly 20% of respondents believed British politics is actually less honest than in other countries.

A Guardian/ICM opinion poll taken on the eve of the 1996 Conservative Party conference and published in October 1996 revealed overwhelming public support for measures to reform and regulate payments to political parties and MPs. More than 70% of respondents felt it should be a criminal offence for an MP not to disclose outside income in the Register of MPs interests. Nine out of ten respondents felt political parties should be required by law to reveal the sources and levels of funds received as donations. However 75% of respondents opposed the public funding of political parties.

The raising of serious constitutional questions and widespread public concern at the damage being done to the democratic system were the reasons given by the leaders of the Labour Party and Liberal Democrats when they urged John Major, then the Conservative Prime Minister, to set up a public inquiry headed by a distinguished judge to investigate the 'cash for questions' affair. Both opposition party leaders felt the proposed enquiry by Sir Gordon Downey, would be inadequate, as he had insufficient powers.

Although the majority of sleaze allegations have involved Tory MPs, in the minds of voters it would appear all politicians and 'the system' are tarred with the same brush. For example, The Guardian/ICM poll revealed that nearly 70% of respondents believed MPs of all parties were being paid by lobbyists, a ludicrously high figure.

This public distrust of politicians is mirrored elsewhere in Europe. During the 1990s the word 'Politikverdrossenheit' entered the German language - literally a sullenness or apathy towards politics. A number of explanations have been advanced to account for this malaise in German politics, including the blandness and incompetence of politicians when facing major problems in the country, not least the reunification of Germany.

138

However, a major contributory factor is the rise in the number of political scandals. These scandals have largely revolved around the 'perks' enjoyed by politicians by way of allowances and salaries and the abuse of public office for personal financial gain. The justification given for self-awarded pay rises was similar to that given in Britain: unless salaries were paid at the right level, individuals of the right calibre would not be attracted to public life. But such rises attracted unfavourable attention from a population regularly exhorted to tighten their belts to meet the costs of reunification.

Sleaze allegations led to the fall of Lothar Spath, the prominent CDU Minister - President of Baden Wuthenberg, who resigned in 1992 following allegations he had received gifts from businessmen. Max Striebl, a Bavarian CSU politician, was forced to resign in 1993 as a result of the "Amigo affair", where it was alleged he had received holidays and travel facilities from businessmen. Known as the 'letterhead affair' it led to the resignation of Jurgen Mollemann, Federal Minister for the Economy, when it was revealed he had used official notepaper to advertise his brother-in-law's business.

In October 1996, mainstream parties in France stood accused of failing ordinary voters, many of whom expressed their anger by voting for the Communist or National Front candidates in a by-election near Marseilles, caused by the bankruptcy and conviction for corruption of Bernard Tapie, the socialist tycoon. The turn-out of 41% and the surprising first round result was a direct result of a loss of confidence by voters following a number of corruption scandals. "The result shows the advanced state of decomposition of French political life," said Alain Madelin, the former finance minister. "It illustrates a deep gulf between politicians and the everyday concerns of French people."

After Antonio Di Pietro, the investigating magistrate from Milan, began the 'clean hands' investigation in Italy, there were 3,000 investigations into corrupt links between politicians and businessmen, including investigations dealing with the affairs of five former Prime Ministers. Systematic corruption which was behind the funding of political parties has created an impenetrable conspiracy. An analysis by one leading newspaper in March 1994 read: "Permanent office led to corruption and decay. The state became an instrument of patronage and votes.

Italy acquired as a result, the biggest most bloated state in Western Europe... its own version of Eastern Europe's nomenclature... the governing parties and their politicians, grew rich off a system of 'tangenti', or kick-backs, which became rife in contracts for the public sector... The legal state became enmeshed with the illegal state and Italy became a country of intrigue, political violence and dirty tricks."

THIS RISING TIDE of sleaze throughout the developed nations of the world has weakened public faith in democratic institutions and promoted a withdrawal by the electorate from the democratic system. It is most pronounced where the democratic process and its supporting institutions are weak or 'still-born', such as in fledgling democracies or despotic societies where political power is concentrated in governing cliques. It is all too easy for predators to seize control of the reigns of power.

Mikhail Gorbachev's announcement that the Soviet Union would undergo a period of perestroika (restructuring) following his assumption of the post of General Secretary of the Communist Party in 1985, was a cause for concern for many in that country, not least the corrupt. Gorbachev had been a close associate of Yuri Andropov, who before his death in 1984 had begun to pursue corrupt officials linked to organised crime, drawing upon his experience as a former head of the KGB.

In 1986 Gorbachev authorised a renewed campaign following the consolidation of his power base within the party. In 1987 Leonid Brezhnev, son-in-law of the former Soviet leader, and Yuri Churbanov, deputy Minister of the Interior of the USSR, were arrested. Churbanov's trial implicated Brezhnev himself, along with his representatives in the Republic and many of his family and friends.

Gorbachev then gave Boris Yeltsin the task of tackling corruption in Moscow by appointing him head of the city's Party Committee. It is said that Yeltsin changed the staff of the Committee three times and nearly 2,000 employees were arrested for misuse of power. So great was the scale of corruption in the former Soviet Union that no border could be discerned between officials and criminals - 'korruptsiya'. In Uzbekistan in the late 1980s, almost all the regional and district party bosses were suspected of misappropriation of official funds and trafficking in contraband as part of the black economy.

Economic disorder had arisen from the Soviet Union's programme of militarisation, bias to heavy industry and chaotic financial administration.

In the days of Stalin, the cruelty of the state held the system in place and kept corruption and fraud at an tolerable level. The liberalisation of the Khruschev regime, however, saw the beginning of the pillage of state property. In turn low official wages encouraged even the lower echelons to flesh out their incomes by theft or corruption. An underground economy developed, known as 'nishinstvo', a poverty so desperate that one loses shame and moral sense.

In 1991 it was estimated that half the income of the average government functionary in the USSR consisted of bribes. By that same point, 20,000 police officers were being dismissed per year for collusion with organised crime.

What then has happened since the fall of communism? Many of the criminals now masquerade as entrepreneurs and the culture of corruption which was engendered under the old system still exists, with many of the officials and politicians playing a role.

Following the failed military putsch of 1991, the new government strove to assert its authority. Their first step was to secure the assets of the state, but they found that capital had been spirited away to foreign banks and that state enterprises had been used as the private banking houses of shadowy groups. These were run, for the most part, by former nomenklatura (the official political administrative and intellectual élite). As the economy falls apart, corruption is rampant in the former Soviet Union at all levels in society.

Corruption within the armed forces has become a huge problem with numerous reports of military units selling weapons, vehicles and supplies, simply to buy food and fuel because salaries have not been paid for months. There have even been reports of officers entering into partnership with organised crime elements, leading to potential scenarios only envisaged in the minds of thriller writers: major criminals armed with weapons of mass destruction holding the world to ransom.

According to a CIA report entitled, 'Prospects for Unsanctioned use of Russian Nuclear Weapons', security measures to prevent the unauthorised use of Russian nuclear weapons can no longer be relied upon. "Conspiracies within nuclear armed units have became a concern as living conditions and morale have deteriorated in the military, even among élite nuclear submariners, nuclear warhead handlers and the SRF (Strategic Rocket Forces)," said the report.

Another report by the Centre for Defence Studies in 1996 warned: "Corruption and organised crime have penetrated every part of Russian life. The transport of nuclear materials is often not secure and does not always conform even to Russian health and safety regulations... the leakage of nuclear materials therefore constitutes a serious international security problem."

This warning proved to be accurate when in November 1996 it emerged radioactive material had been removed from the Radon factory and nuclear waste disposal site near the village of Tolstoy - Yurt, north of the Chechen capital of Grozny. It was suspected demoralised Russian soldiers pilfered the nuclear stocks to sell on the black market as material capable of producing a 'dirty bomb' which would be a potent terrorist weapon. On other occasions Russian soldiers have been killed when warheads they were trying to steal have exploded. But where they failed, have any succeeded?

The cynical would say corruption and organised crime are the only things that work in the brave new post communist world of the former Soviet Union and its satellite states. Bulgaria hovers on the brink of economic disaster due to dwindling foreign reserves and hyper inflation. Again, groups linked to former senior officials within the governing Bulgarian Socialist Party are suspected of siphoning off resources from state enterprises to private cartels and then salting away the plunder in foreign bank accounts. These outflows of unidentified capital are alleged to be the main reason underlying the rise in demands for foreign currency and the depreciation of the local currency. The resultant rise in consumer prices by about 20% each month only puts pressure on the lower paid officials to accept bribes or pillage state property to survive.

Similar experiences can be had in African countries such as Zaire, where from the moment of arrival, the visitor is made aware government employees do not earn enough to live on and progress depends upon the donation of "un petit cadeau". Disintegrating roads are left unrepaired and the commercial infrastructure has disappeared due to poor communications and an underground economy based upon graft. Policemen, customs officials, doctors and others working in the public domain are all involved. Nobody is surprised when a school reports a 100% pass rate in examinations, they just wonder how much the examiners were paid.

One prominent Tanzanian writer has called for a 'revolution for honesty', arguing that corruption 'stands out as the greatest impediment to development.' At the same time, the Swedish Ambassador to Tanzania, Thomas Palme, spoke out against the misuse of public funds and the demands for kickbacks from foreign firms competing for contracts. His considered verdict was that: "the country has now been brought to a stage where choice must be made between corruption and development. The two are incompatible."

Similar conclusions were reached by KPMG, the giant accountancy and consultancy organisation. Studies showed that a growing number of UK companies refuse to conduct business in Eastern Europe and the former Soviet Union, due to rising levels of fraud and malpractice. Nigeria is highlighted as the worst risk of all for businessmen and three quarters of UK respondents cited Nigeria as a country in which they would not do business.

A RADICAL solution for the ills of sub-Saharan Africa has been proposed by Robert Whelan, Assistant Director of the Institute of Economic Affairs, health and welfare unit. Whelan proposes wholesale privatisation in African countries to combat corrupt regimes. He harks back to the charter companies of the imperial past, such as the British South Africa Company and the Imperial East Africa Company, which played a significant role in guaranteeing law and order, defence and a stable infrastructure. Whelan argues that consortia formed from international businesses could tax the population at levels outlined in a manifesto published as a prelude to democratic elections.

Many will think that Whelan's prescription is a bitter pill to swallow but his warnings have to be taken seriously. "Africa is the pit into which we pour our futile good intentions," he says, dismissing proposals by the International Monetary Fund to use $5 billion of its resources to redeem the debts of a number of African countries. "All that will do is show that fraud, corruption and improvidence will be well rewarded and good government will get nothing."

Regardless of whether 'sleaze' denotes political practices which are seen as 'dodgy' at one end of the scale, or grand corruption at the other, it has the same effect - it damages democracy. Either participants in the political process withdraw as the populace forms the belief that politicians are self serving, or, in developing nations, the greater population cannot play a full role in the political process due to despotism or weak democratic institutions.

In turn, a weakening or absence of democratic checks and balances allows predatory forces to infiltrate the system in the form of systemic corruption and organised crime. As such damaging forces gain in strength, the state economy is further weakened to the point where corrupt practice is widespread: the population at large are forced to resort to illegal methods in order to survive. A further effect comes from a lack of investment as financiers fear a lack of stability and higher operating costs (the cost of pay-offs and graft) and thus withdraw from the market. Those in public life may have rich pickings, but for the rest of the population there is only further hardship. Corruption is only good for a selfish few.

The detrimental effects of corruption on developing countries were discussed recently in The Financial Times, the highly-respected business newspaper based in London. The newspaper suggested that corruption has become so deeply rooted in **Russia** that it is jeopardising the development of a free-market economy and putting many Russians off the idea of democracy. A report to the Russian government detailed systematic theft of property by top managers costing tens of trillions of roubles.

In December 1994 press reports dubbed **India** as a land where corruption posed the single greatest obstacle to foreign investment and economic development. Official corruption was cited as one of the major concerns of foreign investors, bleeding funds from programmes intended to develop the economic infrastructure.

In March 1996 a **Thai** opinion poll found that corrupt politicians and corrupt bureaucrats were considered to differ only in that corrupt politicians, fearing a limited career, tended to take more over a shorter period. Thai public opinion is that corruption in public life was widespread - the Police Department topped the league table as the most corrupt government agency.

An example of corruption directly affecting the poorest occurred in **Ecuador** in early 1996. More than 90,000 tonnes of rice, missing as a result of a corruption scandal, contributed to a significant rise in the price of rice - in a country where it forms a major part of the staple diet. The rice disappeared from private warehouses used by the state run distribution company.

In July 1994 John McFarlane, head of Standard Chartered Bank's **Asian** trade activities, stated the bank would not engage in business in countries where bribes were necessary to conduct business. One banking analyst retorted: "If Standard really means it intends to withdraw from countries where corruption is endemic, it would have to quit more than half of the world." It is a depressingly realistic comment.

144

Chapter Twelve

WHISTLEBLOWERS

*"The only thing necessary for the triumph of evil is for good
men to do nothing." Edmund Burke*

WHEREVER there is secrecy there will be leaks. Even in countries where more open approaches to government are pursued there will be matters kept from public view. Sometimes the reasons may be defensible, other times the reasons are to avoid embarrassment or because a culture of secrecy exists. In these situations, someone will occasionally decide to shed some light.

Whistleblowers play a crucial role in the uncovering of corruption, as well as fraud, crime, environmental damage, consumer affairs and social injustice. But they are rarely rewarded for their actions, and the career prospects of those who act are usually blighted.

Clive Ponting, a senior civil servant in the Ministry of Defence, was prosecuted in 1985 under the Official Secrets Act for revealing details of the sinking of the Argentine battleship 'General Belgrano' during the Falklands conflict. He was acquitted when the jury obviously decided he had acted in the best interests of the public.

Recent government initiatives in Britain have enlisted the help of whistleblowers to prevent crime, fraudulent social security claims and tax evasion. In December 1996 Brian Hayes, the Metropolitan Police Deputy Commissioner, announced the introduction of an anti-corruption hotline called 'The Right Line', throughout the 'Met' as a symbol of a determination to prevent corruption.

In taking this action, the Met has recognised wealthy criminals exist with the potential to subvert the investigative and judicial process through improper relationships with police officers. "The number of the new internal telephone line will be displayed in offices across the Met and is a symbol of our determination to stamp out any hint of corruption," said Hayes. "We need to encourage a philosophy where every member of the MPS (Metropolitan Police Service) sees it as their duty to draw dishonest or unethical behaviour to attention. The rotten apple causes enormous damage to the reputation of the MPS and must be dealt with."

In Lord Nolan's second report into standards in public life in May 1996, he proposed a code of practice which would allow worries to be raised inside organisations rather than through leaks to the press or MPs. He further recommended that such a code should stress malpractice is taken seriously and should also offer confidentiality to informants. As a counterbalance it was felt that penalties for the making of false and malicious allegations should also be available.

In apparent opposition to proposals to free up the reporting of possible misconduct or corrupt practice in local government, Westminster City Council (who were facing a huge 'homes for votes' scandal) asked Lord Nolan to introduce penalties to allow the prosecution of councillors, officials and journalists who leak confidential documents. The scandal which forms a backdrop to these recommendations involved allegations that Tory councillors and officials in Westminster Council gerrymandered electoral wards through the letting of council properties to people who would be likely to vote for their party. Dame Shirley Porter, the former council leader, and five other councillors and officials face a £31 million surcharge over the allegations at the time of writing, but they are appealing to the High Court in an effort to have the verdict overturned.

Apart from wanting whistleblowers punished, the same council also proposed the abolition of surcharges imposed upon members found responsible for causing financial loss to the authority, looser rules for the acceptance of gifts and hospitality by authority members and the right of councillors to participate in the making of local authority decisions which might benefit them.

The submission made by Westminster was seized upon by the press because of the background scandal and this apparent attempt to make malpractice even more difficult to expose. It is regrettable that in the United Kingdom no proper procedure exists for right-minded people to expose their fears and suspicions.

The nearest the UK has come to the introduction of a formal structure for the voicing of concern is a charity established to advise whistleblowers, 'Public Concern at Work'. During 1995, the charity received more than 1500 inquiries, including 600 requests for legal help. Of these requests, 312 were classified as public concerns relating to matters endangering the public or threatening the public interest, and thus qualifying for free legal assistance.

Public Concern at Work has been approached by workers involved in commerce, financial services, charities, the care sector, manufacturing, local government and the civil service. As well as advising on fraud and corruption, the charity has dealt with inquiries about unethical behaviour, discrimination, environmental matters and anti-competitive practices.

The Piper Alpha disaster, in which an oil rig caught fire, led to rules to protect employees who wish to raise Health and Safety matters and a pensions scandal involving Robert Maxwell and his Mirror Group made it easier for people to raise relevant concerns. However, Guy Dehn, director of Public Concern at Work, sees a great need for proper legal protection of whistleblowers who act in the public interest.

One opportunity has been lost. In 1996, Dan Touhig MP introduced the Public Disclosure Bill to Parliament. The proposals were intended to reassure employees their careers would not be damaged by raising suspicions of activities threatening the public interest, provided matters were raised internally first. Employees would not be protected if found to be acting in bad faith or if the story had been sold to a newspaper. For those who followed the rules and were punished, injunctions were to have been available as well as means to seek compensation for loss of earnings and damage to reputation. Despite strong support from MPs, Public Concern at Work, the TUC and others, the bill was 'talked out' of Parliament, with MPs filibustering to prevent a vote being taken.

Such legislation has been enacted in other parts of the world. The Protected Disclosures Act 1994 came into operation in the state of New South Wales, Australia, on 1st March 1995. A 'protected disclosure' is defined as: "Information given voluntarily by a public official about conduct in a New South Wales public authority relating to corruption, maladministration or serious and substantial waste of public money."

The Act makes it a criminal offence to take 'detrimental action' against a person for making such a disclosure. Detrimental action includes injury, damage, loss, intimidation, dismissal or disciplinary action. The Act also protects whistleblowers against liability for actions which may be taken against them such as defamation, breach of secrecy or confidentiality agreements.

Provisions to encourage whistleblowing in the United States go further through attempts to actually encourage the reporting of fraud and corrupt practices. The Federal False Claims Act enacted in 1863, and substantially amended in 1986, allows private citizens with knowledge of fraud practised against the US government to bring legal actions on behalf of the government against the perpetrators, and to receive a share of the proceeds of any successful action for damages. To date, recoveries on behalf of the US Government under such provisions have exceeded $800 million, mostly for defence procurement frauds. A number of US States have enacted similar state legislation to protect their own state-funded programmes from fraud and corruption.

Chester Walsh was a marketing executive for General Electric in Israel when he discovered that several of his bosses at the Cincinnati headquarters of the company were falsifying documents. It was being done in collaboration with an Israeli Air Force General, Rami Dotan, to secure US foreign military sales aid and profits were channelled into Swiss bank accounts.

After making many requests for a transfer from Israel, his request was finally granted and Walsh told other General Electric executives of the fraud that was being practised. Following intervention from General Dotan, investigations were dropped and through a lawyer Walsh then filed a claim under the False Claims Act.

FBI investigators found the conspirators had stolen $26.5 million from the US military aid programme. In March 1991 General Dotan was convicted in Israel of bribery, theft and conspiracy to kidnap an Israeli defence ministry official who had assisted the investigation. He was sentenced to 13 years in prison. General Electric pleaded guilty to four charges of diverting millions of dollars of US military aid. The company agreed to pay $9.5 million in fines and to reimburse $59.5 million to the US Treasury.

What of the whistleblower Chester Walsh? On 4th December, 1992 he was awarded $13.4 million under the provisions of the False Claims Act. It was a powerful incentive to others to take a similar stand.

In the United Kingdom, one of the checks and balances in the system is the press but how effective is it? The case of Bennett and Others v Guardian Newspapers Ltd illustrates the problems. The Guardian published two articles in 1992 about investigations at Stoke Newington police station and the transfer of eight unnamed officers to other stations. The investigation eventually involved the Police Complaints Authority and the focus of inquiries were described by the Metropolitan Police Commissioner, Sir Peter Imbert, as "the most serious allegations of police corruption for 20 years".

Despite the fact the officers were not named and that a newspaper should be free to comment upon events of such public importance, the eight officers sued for libel, supported in their action by the Police Federation. The case progressed to trial with, by then, only five officers pursuing actions.

The newspaper had been hoping to argue qualified privilege in its defence, in that the community had an equal interest in receiving the information as the newspaper had in publishing it. If that defence had been available, the prosecution would have had to prove the Guardian article was malicious or reckless as to whether what was published was true or not. In that event, the cases would almost certainly have never been brought but that defence was denied to The Guardian by the trial judge. In the end the jury found in favour of The Guardian but the paper was put to much trouble and expense in defending itself.

In the US the situation would have been wholly different, thanks largely to another case involving the police and dating back to 1964. The case of New York Times v Sullivan of that year, a case ruled upon by the Supreme Court on appeal, fundamentally changed the law of libel in the United States, swinging the balance in the favour of the media. It allowed it to comment upon events of public importance, to the extent that false statements made in the heat of debate are allowed if not made maliciously. The judgement read: "Debate on public issues should be uninhibited, robust and wide open and... it may well include vehement, caustic and sometimes unpleasantly sharp attacks on government and public officials."

The European Court of Human Rights has also upheld the principle that public figures should display a degree of resilience in the face of criticism and justified comment. In the case of Lingens v Austria before the court, it was held that a libel award made against a commentator was contrary to the spirit of Article 10 of the European Convention on Human Rights as it deterred the media from commenting freely on matters of public interest and importance. In short, libel laws in Britain are arguably a hindrance in the system of public debate - something not present in other countries.

In 1993 a newspaper managed to achieve one small victory. The House of Lords held that in a democratic society a government body had to be open to criticism uninhibited by the laws of libel, and therefore could not sue. The case involved The Sunday Times newspaper, Derbyshire County Council, its leader David Bookbinder and the businessman Owen Oyston. The newspaper paid damages to the two men, but its argument that the council could not sue was upheld by the Law Lords. Lord Keith felt that such actions should not be brought because they 'place an undesirable fetter on freedom of speech'. Lord Keith also extended the reasoning to 'any governmental body exercising governmental functions' and 'a corporate public authority'. But such a ruling did not, of course, preclude public officials from suing for libel if they were individually defamed, in contrast to the position in the US.

A number of issues still need to be clarified. Are Quangos 'public bodies' and thereby not entitled to sue for libel? Whereas the Prison Service is a government body, are companies supplying the privatised prisoner escort services under similar restrictions? The clear distinction drawn by Lord Keith has become blurred and puts the journalist once more on guard.

A free press allows challenges to be mounted to political orthodoxy, informed debate on public issues and provides a bulwark against misconduct, waste, injustice and corruption. The obsession with secrecy in government in the Britain, by politicians of all colours, begs the question, are we not possessed of a sufficiently mature democracy to allow the people to be supplied with all relevant information and to debate policy openly?

Not only are the people not supplied with information, but, for the most part, MPs - the elected representatives of the people - are inadequately informed. In December 1996 Conservative MP James Pawsey commented during a debate on 'open government' that the time had come for the introduction of a Freedom of Information Act, such as instituted by many other countries, including member states of the Commonwealth.

"I am a convert," he said, "because I want to see additional power placed in the hands of ordinary citizens. Freedom of Information results in better informed public debate," and provided, "less opportunity for mistakes to be swept under ministerial carpets or under departmental carpets".

The Tory MP Richard Shepherd supported this view, taking as his example the sale of Ministry of Defence housing, which he described as public matters: "What is for sale and the conditions attached to it are a matter of public knowledge. For how else can you assure people that you have done it in an open, above-board way and achieved the best possible price?"

The introduction of a Freedom of Information Act has been a long standing constitutional pledge of the Labour Party, featuring in every party manifesto since 1983. In February 1997, Derek Foster, the former Labour Shadow Public Service Minister, re-stated his commitment to its introduction during the first year of a Labour government, adding: "The new act will be a bold statement of intent... It will form the cornerstone of our new contract with the people."

Tony Blair, Labour leader and Prime Minister, has reaffirmed this pledge on a number of occasions, notably in a John Smith Memorial lecture, and legislation is now awaited. The intention is to go much further that the former Conservative Government's 'Code Of Practice On Open Government', introduced in 1994 giving a statutory right of access to personal files. It was invoked on 1,353 occasions during 1995.

An act would demonstrate a greater commitment to transparency in public life. It would provide for a statutory right of access to most official documents. If experience in other countries is to be used as a guide, the provisions of new legislation would be used far more than those of the Code of Practice.

British secrecy in areas of public life has been recognised by others, notably the Guild of Editors, The Campaign for Freedom of Information, Liberty and the pressure group Article 19 which issued a 'Joint Declaration on Open Government and Open Justice' in January 1996.

The declaration called for: a Freedom of Information Act to apply to central and local government and the National Health Service; the restoration and extension of statutory rights of public scrutiny over bodies that perform public services; action to ensure that local government properly and consistently implements existing 'open access' legislation; a review of 'confidentiality clauses' prohibiting employees from speaking out on issues of public concern; a review of data protection legislation that can be used to obstruct genuine investigation of public interest matters; full scale reform of the libel laws and laws of contempt of court; a reversal of extensions to legislation which effectively outlaws the possession of information and the protection of sources. As regards the legal system, the Article 19 called for a greater commitment to open justice with a right of access to court decisions and documents, and the right to publish all court decisions and challenge orders restricting publication.

Democracy depends upon a well-informed population able to engage in public policy without fear of legal retribution, unless accusations are made maliciously, and without being severely hamstrung through a state of ignorance caused by excessive secrecy. Of course, not all government documents may be disclosed; there are matters which must be kept secret for reasons of national security, the effective investigation of crimes or on grounds of economic sensitivity. But secrecy should be the exception rather than the rule in a mature democracy.

During the so-called Matrix Churchill affair in Britain, public interest immunity certificates or 'gagging orders' were signed by Government ministers in efforts to withhold official documents from the courts during the trial of those accused of illegally exporting arms to Iraq. Some of these documents proved the defendants had acted with the knowledge of the Government and were therefore powerful evidence for the defence. The certificates issued, however, could have denied the defence access to this evidence had it not been for the intervention of the trial judge who ordered disclosure. Somewhat belatedly, Government ministers have now conceded that in any future application made for the disclosure of official papers, the document may only be withheld where there is a likelihood of real harm being caused by their release rather than the issue of blanket prohibitions.

The electorate is not something to be courted whenever an election is impending, fed the party line, milked of its votes and then sent back once more to a state of darkness. In an ideal system, every voter would vote on every governmental issue. Because that is not feasible, we elect representatives. Those representatives should be well informed, as should the electorate.

Whistleblowers who make disclosures out of genuine concern for the public interest deserve protection from reprisals and recognition for their public spirit. A greater degree of open government and public debate would lead to a lesser need for those who blow the whistle.

The Committee to Protect Journalists, based in the United States, makes awards to journalists who operate in conditions where their personal safety is endangered. In 1995 one such award went to Veronica Guerin, the Irish investigative reporter assassinated following her investigations into organised crime in Dublin. One of the 1996 nominees J. Jesus Blancornelas, editor in chief of the Zeta newspaper in Tijuana, Mexico, wrote in the Guardian newspaper of London in 1996: "Surviving 40 years of all this has been very hard for me. Especially when the majority of the media are used by politicians to maintain power, [by] big business to shield and protect their interests and [by] drug traffickers to discredit the few honest policemen that there are in Mexico ... To work as a journalist free from interference, to survive violence as well as attack by bureaucratic red tape and lawsuit, and to retire for reasons of age is truly a feat in Mexico."

Chapter Thirteen

COUNTER MEASURES

"Long is the way,
And hard, that out of hell leads
up to the light"
John Milton

The neutralisation of sleaze and blatant corruption can involve 'stings', undercover operations, 'shakedowns' and 24-hour police surveillance. But it also requires stern political will, open democratic systems with strong, participating parties, and interest groups, free judicial systems and strategic planning. Much of what is discussed in this book does not fall within the criminal law and is therefore not capable of being prosecuted as corruption. But even if it were, prosecution is not the only answer.

Codes of conduct (with appropriate sanctions), greater access to information and mass participation in the political process are all bulwarks against the abuse of power. International abuses require the implementation of similar reforms on a supranational level. Nowhere does the maxim 'prevention is better than cure' ring truer than in the prevention of abuse of trust, for although short term campaigns grab headlines and sacrifice a few scapegoats, they do not get to the root of the problem.

In Britain, the Nolan Committee on Standards in Public Life concentrated on how British MPs might face conflicts arising from outside interests and their parliamentary duties. As a result of its deliberations, the committee has formulated its 'Seven Principles of Public Life', applicable to all public officials, which to the observer might seem an obvious code to follow: Selflessness - Public officials should take decisions only in the public interest and not so as to obtain benefit for themselves, family or friends; Integrity - Holders of office should not place themselves under financial or other obligations that might influence the discharge of official duties; Objectivity - In making public appointments, awarding contracts etc., office holders should make choices on merit; Accountability - Holders of public office are accountable for their decisions; Openness - Office holders should be as open as possible about decision and actions taken. Information should only be withheld in the public interest; Honesty - Office holders should declare any private interests relating to public duties and attempt to resolve them to protect the public interest; Leadership - Holders of public office should support the principles by example and through leadership.

The committee went on to recommend the publication of codes of conduct based upon these same seven principles throughout many areas of public life. Having recommended that codes should be established for those in public life, the committee considered the problem of enforcement, especially in relation to MPs.

As already discussed, the Nolan Committee recommended the appointment of a Parliamentary Commissioner for Standards to supervise a Register of Members Interests, advise on the Code of Conduct, receive complaints about MPs and investigate allegations. The Commissioner has the power to dismiss complaints, find them proven and remedy the matter with the MP involved, or refer them for further investigation by the seven member Committee of Privileges. The Committee of Privileges normally sits in public and can recommend penalties.

To the observer, these reformed procedures still smack of the old boys network and the exclusion of independent, outside supervision. However, a number of significant changes have become evident. Proposals have been made for a new code which would define ministers' responsibilities to Parliament and set a scale by which their openness may be judged.

A draft resolution on accountability heard by the Commons Public Service Committee in January 1997 stressed the importance of ministers giving 'accurate and truthful information', with any errors to be corrected at the earliest opportunity. Any instance of knowingly misleading the House would lead to an expectation of resignation. Any refusal to provide information would be permissible 'only when disclosure would not be in the public interest'.

The cynical might say that semantics have always allowed adroit ministers to slide out of a tight spot. But MPs and others who give evidence before the disciplinary committee on Standards and Privileges will, henceforth, give such evidence on oath, relegating to the history books the time-honoured custom that all MPs are treated as 'honourable members' and 'totally trustworthy'. Any witness found lying risks being charged with perjury, though such a prosecution would require a vote in the House of Commons to remove his or her parliamentary immunity from prosecution.

The last time an MP was jailed by Parliament was more than a century ago, partly because the 1689 Bill of Rights causes problems for any prosecution of an MP arising out of his or her Parliamentary activities. As part of the process of reform, the Nolan Committee sought a clarification in relation to the law of bribery as it applied to MPs.

A Home Office consultative document, prepared as a result, put forward three options: to make MPs subject to criminal law by waiving the protection of the 1689 Bill of Rights in cases of bribery; Parliament to decide which breaches of the criminal law should be a matter of privilege; and criminal proceedings against an MP or peer to be subject to a full vote in Parliament. The new Labour Home Secretary, Jack Straw, has announced his support for moves to make MPs liable under new bribery legislation.

Consideration is finally being given to the development of laws which would enable MPs to be prosecuted for bribery, thus overcoming the legal anachronism. In another move, seen as an attempt to curb fraud and corruption in relation to public money, the Conservative government announced in February 1997 that Sir John Bourn, the Comptroller and Auditor General, would head a working party to identify the best ways of monitoring £15 billion of public money passing to such organisations as housing associations, training and enterprise councils, universities and private contractors.

This external inspection was urged by the Audit Commission, whose Chief Executive believed 'a rigorous public audit regime should apply to all bodies which are responsible for spending public money, whatever their formal status'. Sir John Bourn has argued for such an extension to his duties, seeing it as a nonsense the European Court of Auditors may follow European Union funds expended in the United Kingdom, whereas he did not hold similar powers in relation to public funding.

Not to be outdone, the Labour Opposition, announced that Sir John Bourn - as Comptroller and Auditor General under a future Labour government - would be given wide ranging powers to vet contracts and public appointments prior to their being made public. These proposals immediately earned Sir John the unofficial title of 'Sleazebuster General'. The view was taken by Labour that supervision of government programmes had not improved at the same pace as the delivery of these programmes, which had undergone radical change during the 18 years of Tory government. The powers held by the National Audit Office, headed by Sir John Bourn, had not changed from the era when all Government services were provided by government departments without the intervention of public sector contractors.

It was argued the National Audit Office should be given powers to investigate the accounts of private companies providing public services. One example which immediately drew press comments was the passing of public funds in the region of £1 billion per annum to the Housing Corporation, which is currently audited by a private firm, leading to a situation where the National Audit Office cannot, itself, give public reassurance these moneys are being spent efficiently. Other examples are potential audits of the National Lottery, the privatisation of rail services and the sale of Ministry of Defence homes. In a further radical departure, it was also proposed the NAO would become proactive in ensuring public money is being spent efficiently rather than waiting for requests to examine alleged impropriety.

It was also proposed that all manifestations of central government should fall within the remit of the redefined NAO, including the dreaded Quangos. A promise was made that, under the new Labour regime, all public appointments to them would be advertised and a list of all members would be placed on the Internet for ready access. Political affiliation of members together with offices held during the previous five years and any political donations made over £5,000 would be put into the public domain. This latter proposal contrasted with the Tory Government's refusal to provide this same information despite requests from Peter Kilfoyle MP. Kilfoyle has a passionate interest in Quangos and has asked in excess of 800 parliamentary questions in his attempts to discover the membership of all Government appointed trusts, advisory committees and funding agencies. A request by Kilfoyle for the production of an annual directory of Quango members, with their addresses, remuneration, period of office and political and pecuniary interests, was refused by William Waldegrave, who at the time was Minister for Open Government.

AMERICA is waging war on corruption. In the last two decades nearly 15,000 people have been convicted under the federal corruption statutes. In embracing a more searching and pro-active role for the National Audit Office, both Conservative and Labour parties in Britain could do far worse than study controversial procedures adopted there. In Illinois, it was Operation Gambit; in Tennessee it was Rocky Top; South Carolina had Operation Lost Trust, and Chicago had Operation Silver Shovel. These investigations into political and commercial corruption 'took down' hundreds of federal, state and local officials.

Investigators attribute the prevalence of corruption partly to the enormous sums needed to secure elected office in the US, which makes incumbents beholden to special interest groups, and partly to the increased willingness of the federal authorities to tackle sleaze. By using the same lateral ingenuity which led to the conviction of Al Capone decades before, FBI and other investigators are now using offences such as extortion, mail fraud (a serious crime in the US) and racketeering, to target everyone from civil servants to county sheriffs. For example, the Justice Department moved against Mel Miller, the Democratic Speaker of the New York Assembly and a well-known Democrat at a national level, who was indicted by a federal jury on charges of mail fraud stemming from property deals.

The wave of undercover operations can be traced back to 1977, and a sting known as 'Abscam'. An FBI undercover informant posed as a wealthy Arab sheikh and began spreading money around Washington. He trapped several senior politicians who took his bribes and the resulting trials saw a Senator and several Congressmen convicted of corruption. There was, and still is, strong criticism of these undercover operations, the use of 'entrapment' and informants. But according to one US attorney: "Public corruption cases are difficult to investigate and prosecute. You don't have to be an Einstein to figure out that you need an undercover operation to break through that insulation."

Investigators have also been accused of political and racial bias. But then, as one prosecutor, puts it, when the FBI launch a sting operation, "they don't know who is going to turn up. You don't know whether they'll be male, female, white, black, Democrat or Republican."

Others have complained that the Justice Department and the FBI often go after targets for public relations purposes with little likelihood of securing a conviction. "In general, elected public officials who are investigated for political corruption by federal prosecutors, even if ultimately they are not indicted, must spend so much time, effort, personal funds and emotional resources to keep up with the investigators that they cannot do the work for which they were elected," wrote Arthur Maass, a highly-respected Emeritus Professor of Government at Harvard University, in a magazine article.

But when a dispassionate view is taken of the investigations, we can see that those bleating about harassment or entrapment are normally members of the same party as those who are accused. 'There but for the grace of God go I,' said one Democrat councillor who saw several of his colleagues convicted.

WITH AGGRESSIVE new tactics being used by investigators, the message to US state politicians in any of the 50 state capitals seems to be: avoid that smart new lobbyist keen to donate money to your campaign. In State capitals across America, legislators are being caught by hidden cameras accepting bribes from undercover agents and then having their greed put on public display as the grainy videotapes are broadcast on local news.

Not realising they are being filmed, the corrupt speak honestly: "I do deals. My favourite line is, 'What's in it for me'," said one elected official in the state of Arizona who had accepted a bribe from an undercover agent to support casino gambling. He was one of 17 political figures convicted in the sting.

The existence of a causal link between political donations and policy has been argued in a study by California Common Cause (CCC), a group which seeks to reform the current methods of US political financing. CCC gives the example of Tom Bane, a California politician who accepted $513,000 in campaign contributions between 1979 and 1989 from the savings and loans industry (roughly equivalent to British building societies). Bane sponsored a crucial deregulation bill which allowed California savings and loans companies to take financial risks with 100% of their investors money, rather than the 40% which was previously allowed.

Part of the problem in America is the mass of legislation enacted at a local level. State governments are vast and unwieldy bureaucracies nicknamed 'bill mills'. CCC quotes the California state legislature as an example:

they consider more than 7,000 items every year. Because of this mountain of bills and laws, nearly every committee in every state holds some economic power, and politicians always need money, be it for their election campaign or a new Jacuzzi.

The number of political lobbyists has increased commensurate with the increase in legislation. Even a minor bill in a state legislature can have billion dollar implications for, say, an insurance company, so perhaps it is not surprising when that same insurance company decides to spend just a few hundred thousand dollars trying to influence the outcome of a crucial vote in their favour.

THE STING operations are not always centred on high-level corruption and the manipulation of votes in a legislature. Federal operations are also targeted at the lower levels. Take Operation Silver Shovel in Chicago as an example. Alderman Ambrosio Medrano, a popular local politician, was recently trapped by a government informant, convicted of taking bribes and sentenced to 30 months in prison. Medrano provides a useful insight into the behaviour and psychology of an elected politician prepared to be bought.

Allan Streeter, another councillor, approached Medrano while he was standing alone at a City council meeting and told him he had a friend he wanted Medrano to meet. Streeter said: "He's doing business in my ward. He'd like to do business in your ward. Maybe he can be of some help to you. Maybe you can help him." Medrano met the mole, John Christopher (an ex-convict running illegal rubbish dumps, who Medrano knew as Johnny DiVito), over lunch at the Quality Inn restaurant with Streeter. "I remember when I saw him, I thought, "Ohhhhhhh, Jesus," said Medrano. "He looked like a slime-bag. He's got a receding hairline, a deep voice and he talked like he's got marbles in his mouth. All he ever wore was a shirt and slacks. And he was a chain smoker of Marlboro cigarettes."

After Streeter left, Christopher told Medrano he was looking for a site within his ward to make room for a rock crusher. "We can make a lot of money," said Christopher. According to Medrano, Christopher wrote down some figures: "and he said: 'This is what I've done with other people in the past and this is what we've made. This will be yours, what do you think?' I was thinking, man, this guy's really talking fast. You know, he was writing

A grainy shot taken by a hidden video camera of undercover anti-corruption officers from the Hong Kong Independent Commission Against Corruption (ICAC), meeting officials suspected of corruption.

all these things down on a paper napkin. When the conversation was over, he throws the napkin into the water! And it dissolves. Now, what does that usually tell you? What kind of signal is that? The signal there is that this guy is all right. He doesn't want to show anything. You know, he's destroying evidence, OK. So right away that stuck in my head."

After that meeting Christopher would call Medrano every day, but the councillor avoided his calls until the mole started using different names to get him on the phone. Eventually Medrano went to see Christopher in his office, and the mole made him a specific offer: $1,000 a week for his services. Unfortunately for Medrano the FBI had a camera in the ceiling watching his every move.

"I said, 'Yeah, that sounds OK. That sounds fine.' It was OK, so we're on for $1,000 a week. You know, that's how he put it to me. 'We'll pay you for your services. And we'll cut the same deal with anybody else that you can bring us.' So after that, he gave me the money. He put the money on the table and I took it. He just put it on the table in $100 bills. But I never did anything for the money." So how much did he take? "Well, they say I took $31,000. I figure I took about $22,000. Christopher lied... And I can't prove it because he never counted out the money to me [on videotape]."

Not long after that two FBI agents came to see Medrano. "A man and a woman. They said, 'We'd like to talk to you, we think you can provide us with some information. We're doing an investigation on illegal dumping, and we have a clipping here.' It was like a two-year-old clipping, it was in the Sun-Times. The Sun-Times had done an article on this illegal dumping. I said, 'Well, there's not much I can tell you, I mean there's really no illegal dumping in my ward.' I also claimed I didn't know about the companies mentioned in the article. Then they asked me if I had ever met John Christopher, who used aliases of Chris John and John DiVito. I said: 'I don't know. I meet a lot of people'."

When the Feds started talking about the article Medrano began to relax: "I thought, Whew! This is not about me, I have nothing to do with this. But they always would come back to John DiVito or John Christopher. Then the hammer. They said, 'We happen to have a video of an illegal dump site and we think you can identify it for us, would you mind looking at it?' So the woman agent took out this small videocam and hooked it up to my outlet. A strange feeling came over me. Sure enough, I'm on the video. And I just said, "OK, you got me."

I have seen the fear that overcomes people at this point. It is a paralysing terror as they realise that everything they have worked for, fought for, is about to come crashing down around them.

The FBI told Medrano: "That's a good start. That's you on the tape and you've done something wrong. We'd like to talk to you and you have a right to call your attorney. We'd like to ask you some questions. And the only people you have to be concerned with are those people behind you," said the male agent, gesturing to the picture Medrano had of his family behind his desk. According to Medrano they said: "Nobody's going to take care of them, only you can help yourself now. All we're looking for is a little co-operation. We'd like to ask you questions about some people." Medrano talked for three hours. He later pleaded guilty to taking $31,000 in bribes.

Michael Sneed of the Chicago Sun-Times interviewed him about how he had 'tossed away' his dream. "What got me into trouble was me," said

Medrano tearfully. "I have always had a hard time saying no, especially to anyone asking for help."

Beyond Medrano, the FBI investigation widened and investigators now believe it may last until the end of the decade. "This is a very wide-ranging probe, and its tentacles reach in many directions," confirmed James B. Burns, US Attorney. "You go where the leads take you."

The 'tentacles' of the Silver Shovel investigation are more like a web. John Christopher tape-recorded 1,100 separate conversations over the three years he worked under-cover, and according to those who have spoken with the FBI mole, he met and bribed an astonishing number of local and regional officials, businessmen and politicians. "The scope of the investigation is going to be extraordinarily broad, and the net is going to spread over a lot of wards, the entire city and into the suburbs," said one lawyer involved in the case.

But not everyone in Chicago was happy with the Federal government's operation. The Chicago Department of Environment was said to be 'spitting with rage'. The reason? While John Christopher was trapping politicians and local officials for the FBI, he was also working as an illegal rubbish-dumper (a 'fly-tipper', in British parlance). City officials said that about 3,000,000 cubic yards of debris, including some hazardous waste, was dumped on sites operated by the mole himself, or by people who were doing business with him. The same environmental officials estimate that cleaning up the sites will blight Chicago neighbourhoods for years and cost $15 million to remove. Silver Shovel was just one of many highly controversial FBI under-cover operations. In the tiny town of Bolton, North Carolina, the revelation that agents were involved in rigging a referendum on alcohol as part of a political corruption investigation infuriated townspeople and led to calls for the agents to be thrown into prison.

FBI agents posed as crooked businessmen who wanted to open a bar in the town. They paid local leaders to influence a referendum on alcohol - which was banned - as part of an investigation called Colcor, which stood for Columbus County corruption. Colcor led to the conviction of a police chief, senior town officials and a judge.

But the state Board of Elections, which oversees such referenda, said the vote was entirely the idea of the agents, not the residents. It attacked the FBI for entrapment, and overturned the vote - which had gone in favour of the 'businessmen'. The board said the vote was a violation of local citizens' right to free speech and assembly. They even wrote to the Washington in the hope of extracting financial compensation for the citizens.

But how else are these investigations to be conducted if the 'vapour trail' is to be followed? The FBI agents did not force the local councillors to accept bribes - they were known to be corrupt and they gladly accepted them. According to Robert Pence, the FBI agent responsible for North Carolina, the referendum payoffs were "part of the Colcor investigation, which was checked at every juncture and confirmed by attorneys for the FBI and the Justice Department. The reaction into that area was in response to information we received that there were voter irregularities in that area. As far as we're concerned, it was done properly and in compliance with our rules and regulations."

I have every sympathy with the agents. Locals, however, were furious. "I hope they put them in jail," Cephus Duncan, a Bolton councillor said of the undercover agents. "I don't think it [the referendum] would have come up without the FBI."

DRASTIC METHODS have been used elsewhere in the US. In April 1988, the New York State Organised Crime Task Force reported that the construction industry in the city was dominated by corruption and organised crime. Bid rigging, price fixing, the organisation of illegal cartels, bribery, extortion and fraud were all rife. Particularly telling damage had been caused within the City's huge schools construction programme - which has an annual operating budget in excess of $7 billion. In response, the New York State legislature created a new School Construction Authority to meet the challenge. To keep new programmes free from wasteful and criminal practices, the authority sanctioned the establishment of an Office of Inspector General.

The mission of the OIG is: "To protect the Schools Construction Authority from victimisation by racketeering, fraudulent schemes, wasteful practices and all manner of crimes perpetrated by those doing business with, as well as those employed by the SCA..." It adds: "By reducing corruption, fraud and racketeering and by supporting civil suits for the recovery of moneys that have been lost, the OIG will save the SCA money. It should further serve the objective of attracting greater private sector participation in the SCA's construction programmes."

164

In furtherance of this mission, the OIG pursues a three-pronged approach of deterrence, financial recoveries and opportunity 'blocking'. Deterrence is achieved by the creation of a belief within the construction industry that fraudulent practices will be detected and punished. Sophisticated auditing techniques are enforced with investigations, surveillance and 'sting' operations, as well as more traditional law enforcement techniques. Crucially, the fact that corruption is a consensual crime and very hard to prove to the satisfaction of the courts has been acknowledged and for this reason, emphasis is placed upon non-traditional techniques to capture 'real time' evidence through proactive rather than reactive investigation.

As well as criminal sanctions, the OIG presses for civil remedies such as forfeiture, restitution and the award of punitive damages as part of its strategy for making financial recoveries. Depending upon the circumstances, sanctions imposed upon a transgressing organisation may well include debarment or 'blacklisting' in relation to future contract bids.

Opportunity blocking strategies are devised by OIG analysts who draw upon research findings and empirical evidence of corruption and fraud to design methods of preventing abuse. One of the most effective methods employed by the OIG is the pre-qualification programme, which recognises that in most instances public agencies across the world do not assess the background and potential performance of would-be contractors until after bids are submitted. No firm can do business with the New York Schools Construction Authority without having 'prequalified' through a review conducted by the OIG. Such a process allows the SCA to prevent corrupt or inefficient companies from even bidding for contracts. In addition, should a prequalified firm be found to be acting improperly, its prequalification may be rescinded, barring any future participation in the bidding process for SCA contracts. Such a sanction is a powerful economic deterrent. By the Spring of 1995, the OIG had conducted in excess of 3,500 prequalification evaluations which led to the exclusion of over 180 from the contract tendering process. A 'knock-on' effect has been that an SCA debarment has led to other government agencies refusing to do business with these firms.

The 'blacklisting' or debarment of any firm obviously has to be capable of being sustained in a court of law should the firm challenge the decision. On occasions where evidence capable of being admitted leads the OIG to doubt a firm's worthiness, the onus is shifted. The applicant firm is asked to complete a sworn certificate promising that any suspicions held by the OIG are without foundation. If it is later proven these sworn assurances are false, the SCA may cancel all contracts, treat them as having been fraudulently granted and recover all moneys paid while keeping the benefit of any work done.

The scheme is obviously a model to be studied by anybody wishing to minimise fraud, corruption and waste in a particular sector of the economy or a particular industry.

GOVERNMENTS have realised that corruption in international trade is a serious problem which needs to be tackled, yet there has been a noticeable lack of will among the member states of the Organisation for Economic Co-operation and Development (OECD) to force change. In 1976 the OECD agreed a code of conduct for multinational companies, to which most states paid only lip service. Only the US enacted legislation, following a route paved by the Lockheed scandal of the 1970s, when the giant aircraft manufacturer was accused of bribing Japanese officials. The US Foreign Corrupt Practices Act of 1977 banned US companies from paying bribes to win business abroad.

However in March 1996 the 21 member states of Organisation of the American States (OAS) signed the Inter-American Convention against Corruption in Caracas, Venezuela. This initiative requires each signatory country to make bribery of foreign officials a crime and, moreover, one which is extraditable. The Council of Europe was reported to be preparing a similar convention. During the same month, the International Chamber of Commerce approved a series of guidelines urging members to adopt enforceable codes to counter corruption, and calling upon governments to tighten legislation on bribery.

In May 1996 the OECD member states once again considered illicit payments made abroad and agreed to 'criminalise the bribery of foreign officials in an effective and co-ordinated manner'. This had been predicated in April 1996 by the Development Assistance Committee of the OECD, which recommended members should introduce anti-corruption provisions into contracts funded under their aid budgets. In a further move, in June 1997, the OECD published a draft treaty recommending that such legislation be enacted by the end of 1998. At the time of publication ...is draft treaty, offshore bribes were still tax-deductible as legitimate business expenses in 11 OECD member countries.

In October 1996 the World Bank announced that if it found official corruption in projects in which it was involved, it would cancel the project. Firms caught bribing would be 'blacklisted' for appropriate periods. The bank also stated it would work with interested governments to help contain such corruption which might inhibit development.

Between 1977 and 1996 the US stood head and shoulders above the rest of the developed world in taking a stand against foreign bribery. However there are indications this stand is putting it at a commercial disadvantage. A secret US Commerce Department study, prepared with the benefit of intelligence reports in 1994, demonstrated that of 100 deals, worth $45 billion and tracked by US Intelligence agencies, overseas competition used bribes and other illicit advantages to undercut US companies. The result was that foreign companies won 80% of the business.

In the face of such findings, sections of the US business and governmental communities pressed for action to be taken against foreign states playing dirty. The preferred method was through anti-bribery lobbying in international organisations, such as the World Trade Organisation, with a view to drawing up national anti-bribery codes within emerging markets. Any companies doing business in these countries would sign up to these codes with the intention that unofficial, non-binding rules could eventually be enacted into law.

INDEPENDENT of governments, Transparency International (TI), aims to draw attention to the world-wide problem and has lobbied in support of all the measures proposed by the OECD, OAS, ICC, World Bank and European Union. TI was launched in May 1993 by figures from the developed and developing world who were concerned that corruption on a grand scale was dragging poorer countries into ruin. In the ensuing years, there has been pressure upon TI to expand its attentions to take account of growing corruption in the developed nations and the problems faced by the countries in transition from communism in Eastern Europe.

TI sees its strength as resting upon three pillars. Firstly, it fosters co-operation by spanning borders, cultural differences, languages and religions - and seeks to educate and minimise confrontation in its work. Secondly, TI acts through accredited country 'chapters' or branches who take responsibility for anti-corruption programmes in their own areas. The intention is that these should form coalitions of interested parties within their own borders, mimicking the work internationally . Thirdly, TI makes efforts to establish 'Islands of Integrity', realising that given the scale of international corruption, it could prove commercial suicide for a company to unilaterally decide not to pay bribes to win business. As a result TI has initiated attempts to arrange pacts between competitors in well-defined market areas, to stop bribery on an 'I will if you will' basis.

Though it seeks to heighten awareness in the same way as Amnesty International highlights the plight of prisoners of conscience, TI will not investigate individual cases of corruption, its target being institutional reform . In furtherance of this aim, it says it strives to remain outside party politics wherever it operates and takes great care not to fall under partisan control.

One controversial initiative is the production of a 'league table' of corruption in conjunction with the University of Goettingen. This 'Corruption Ranking' is published on the Internet.

The ranking for 1995 presented a list of 41 countries as a 'poll of polls', taking data from surveys of business executives world-wide to gauge the perception of the level of corruption in each of the countries named. Countries are then graded on a scale from 0 to 10 (zero representing a total-ly corrupt country, penetrated by corrupt practices, kickbacks and fraud).

In 1995, New Zealand headed the league table with a score of 9.55, almost totally clean. Languishing at the bottom was Indonesia with a score of 1.94, China with 2.16, Pakistan with 2.25 and Venezuela and Brazil with 2.66 and 2.70 respectively. As a major industrial nation, Italy scored a shameful 2.99. The table for 1996 is printed at the end of this chapter.

What should the countries at the bottom of the TI scale be doing? No two countries will employ exactly the same methods to combat corruption and TI recognises that national chapters need to be given the autonomy to devise their own national programmes. Having said that, there are factors which any anti-national corruption strategy should consider, factors skil-fully cited by Bertrand de Speville, the Commissioner for the Independent Commission Against Corruption in Hong Kong, during an address at the Seventh International Anti-Corruption Conference in Beijing in 1995.

The austere atmosphere of an interview suite, such as this one in Hong Kong, is usually designed to intimidate the suspect.

He said there should be support at the highest level of government for the strategy to combat corruption and that support should recognise the fight against corruption will be a war rather than one set-piece battle. Short term campaigns have no chance of success and may be seen as politically expedient - 'showboating' - having a brief palliative effect. When the campaign finishes, the population is left with the feeling nothing has changed and is more disillusioned than before the campaign began.

The anti-corruption programme must be placed into the hands of agencies commanding the respect of the population and with unblemished reputations for integrity and fair dealing. The agencies should be politically independent. A carefully planned, long term strategy is required which will punish the corrupt, improve systems to prevent corruption and change public attitudes to create an anti-corruption culture.

In the Hong Kong model, this has led to the organisation of the ICAC to promote a three pronged attack upon corruption: investigations - through the Operations Department; prevention - through the efforts of the Corruption Prevention Department; and education - through the Community Relations Department.

De Speville said: "The three tactical approaches, the three departments, are interdependent. In order to achieve maximum efficiency, each department depends on the performance of the others. Thus is the sum of the Commission greater than the sum of its parts."

Public confidence must be both obtained, and retained, with the promise that every allegation of corruption which is pursuable, no matter how small, will be investigated and acted upon. Ignoring a report made in good faith closes the door on future reports from that source.

Confidentiality should be provided for those reporting corruption and all sources should be protected. Powers should be provided to the relevant agencies which recognise the special problem of corruption, where there is often no witness to the corrupt act, save an accomplice. As we shall see the Hong Kong ICAC has substantial, some would say, draconian powers to achieve its ends. Officers are empowered to prevent suspects from disposing of property, to seek court orders, to keep the suspect within the confines of Hong Kong, to examine bank accounts and safe deposit boxes, to require the suspect to provide details of his financial circumstances and to search his premises.

The Hong Kong ICAC model has been replicated through a number of agencies operating throughout the world including the ICAC of New South Wales, Australia (tiny in comparison) and the Directorate on Corruption and Economic Crime of Botswana which was set up in 1994 by a former British Police officer, Graham Stockwell.

The ICAC has been described as the Rolls Royce of anti-corruption agencies and certainly the Hong Kong government has spared no expense in providing the resources required. It is a revelation to anybody interested in anti-corruption work to see it in operation at first hand. I have been fortunate to do so.

TRANSPARENCY INTERNATIONAL POLL OF POLLS

The first number indicates the average score in the surveys. A "1000" indicates a perfectly clean country whereas a "0" refers to a country where business transactions are entirely penetrated by corruption involving immense sums of kickbacks, extortion, fraud, etc. The second number is the amount of surveys in which the particular country has been included (4-10). The third number is the variance of the rankings. A high number indicates a high degree of deviating opinions.

Ranking 1996

Country	Score	Variance	Surveys
1 New Zealand	943	39	6
2 Denmark	933	44	6
3 Sweden	908	30	6
4 Finland	905	23	6
5 Canada	896	15	6
6 Norway	887	20	6
7 Singapore	880	236	10
8 Switzerland	876	24	6
9 Netherlands	871	25	6
10 Australia	860	48	6
11 Ireland	845	44	6
12 Unit.Kingd.	844	25	7
13 Germany	827	53	6
14 Israel	771	141	5
15 USA	766	19	7
16 Austria	759	41	6
17 Japan	705	261	9
18 Hong Kong	701	179	9
19 France	696	158	6
20 Belgium	684	141	6
21 Chile	680	253	7
22 Portugal	653	117	6
23 South Africa	568	330	6
24 Poland	557	363	4
25 Czech Rep.	537	211	4
26 Malaysia	532	13	9
27 South Korea	502	230	9
28 Greece	501	337	6
29 Taiwan	498	87	9
30 Jordan	489	17	4
31 Hungary	486	219	6
32 Spain	431	248	6
33 Turkey	354	30	6
34 Italy	342	478	6
35 Argentina	341	54	6
36 Bolivia	340	64	4
37 Thailand	333	124	10
38 Mexico	330	22	7
39 Ecuador	319	42	4
40 Brazil	296	107	7
41 Egypt	284	664	4
42 Colombia	273	241	6
43 Uganda	271	872	4
44 Philippines	269	49	8
45 Indonesia	265	95	10
46 India	263	12	9
47 Russia	258	94	5
48 Venezuela	250	40	7
49 Cameroon	246	298	4
50 China	243	52	9
51 Bangladesh	229	157	4
52 Kenya	221	369	4
53 Pakistan	100	252	5
54 Nigeria	69	637	4

171

1996 study of corruption by Transparency International and Goettingen University

Different countries and different political systems require a variety of approaches to tackling corruption. President Mkapa of **Tanzania** decided to take dramatic steps to counter the problem in 1995, and voluntarily disclosed - on national radio - the value and source of his personal assets and those of his wife as part of his declared campaign to eradicate corruption in the country. In addition, the President later appointed a nine person team to investigate corruption under the chairmanship of Joseph Warioba, a former Prime Minister. The Anti-Corruption Commission was tasked with making recommendations as to how existing laws and procedures could be improved to prevent corrupt practice.

In the Middle East, anti-corruption campaigners must tread warily. During an anti-corruption drive in March 1996, **Kuwaiti** opposition MPs submitted a bill requiring publication of the identity of any person receiving a commission as a result of the award of state contract. Publication would include the name and occupation of the recipient and any intermediary involved under the proposed legislation. Sadly, the proposal was opposed by a group including a number of wealthy businessmen.

Some of the strongest counter-measures have been taken in **Australia,** where a Royal Commission dealing with the New South Wales Police Service was established in May 1994 following claims by former officers that organised corruption was rife among police ranks. Operating with a reported Aus$100 million ($50 million) budget, teams of investigators, and employing state of the art surveillance techniques, it was announced the Commission would be headed by Justice James Wood. Corruption would be tackled in three phases: first would be a familiarisation phase where an understanding of the structure of the force would be gained and areas of potential corruption identified. Second would come a phase focusing upon special areas of investigation involving corrupt conduct within the service. Third would come a final stage involving police and academics working with the Commission to suggest reforms and strategies to prevent corruption.

Justice Wood said that he would consider the Commission a 'waste of time' if its only achievement was to 'flush out a few crooks'. He hopes the legacy of the Commission will be workable and acceptable structures to take the New South Wales Police Service into the next century.

The operation seems to be going well. Peter Ryan, the former chief constable of Norfolk, England, was thrown in at sharp end in 1996 to take operational control of the campaign, and appears to have weeded-out many of the most corrupt officers among the 13,000 strong force.

When Ryan arrived in Sydney he was confronted by a force that had become a national joke. More than 200 officers were subsequently found to have criminal records, there was rampant criminality among the force, and there was even evidence of police-run paedophile rings. Despite a smear campaign against 'the bloody Pom', Ryan purged the force's senior officers and disbanded the police Special Branch, which had been amassing top secret reports and files on judges, lawyers, politicians and campaigners. The Royal Commission used hidden cameras concealed in television sets, car ashtrays, roofs and clothing to uncover the network of corruption among the force. Such were the effects of the investigations into sleaze and sexual behaviour that at least 10 witnesses committed suicide.

Chapter Fourteen

THE
CHINA
SYNDROME

"Who overcomes
By force, hath overcome but half his foe"
John Milton

IN CHINA, where local mayors and officials often enjoy near-dictatorial
powers in their towns, rampant corruption is a direct product of the
one-party system. According to Li Weimin, a dissident who founded the
underground China Freedom and Democracy Party, corruption is endemic
because the Communist Party "allows no restrictions on or supervision of
its powers. Fighting corruption means fighting itself".

Recent years have seen an explosion of corruption as the nation is
confronted through the media of television and films by the benefits of
materialism and wealth. The Chinese Procurator-General, Zhang Siqing,
has admitted law enforcement officials are dealing with nearly 200,000
complaints of corruption every year.

China's most senior judicial officials have recently called for increased
spending on anti-corruption units, heavier penalties, and quicker trials. In
1994, the most recent year for which records are available in the West, the
Chinese judiciary handled 30,793 cases of corruption, bribery and embezzlement, an increase of nearly 70% on the previous year. Penalties are
harsh: 20,186 men and women were convicted and 6,372 received jail
sentences of at least five years, or, as we learned earlier, the death penalty.

As part of a campaign to dissuade the public from involvement in
corruption, office and factory workers have been shown videos of corruption cases. But apart from warning them of the dangers, the videos have
also shown the public the scandalous aspects of the lives of those in the
Communist Party who rule them. Dissent is hardly surprising when the
videos show senior party officials spending $2,000 or $3,000 on a banquet

or tipping a karaoke bar hostess $1,000 for singing a particular song.

The anti-corruption drive - it is not yet a national campaign - has already claimed senior party officials. Chen Xitong, the head of the Beijing Communist party and a senior Communist Party Politburo member was recently arrested. Wang Baosen, the Beijing Executive Vice Mayor, committed suicide rather than face the disgrace - and a possible death sentence - of a corruption trial. Next on the list of targets for the zealous anti-corruption police was another senior Beijing politician who was close to Chen and who oversaw numerous large construction projects, including the Asian Games Village - built quickly and at huge expense for the Asian Games of 1990.

Even while the village was under construction the gossip at Beijing dinner tables was of the huge bribes and back-handers being paid by construction companies for a chance to work on the project. The Mayor of Beijing came under suspicion and police investigation when one of his aides was implicated in a case involving a firm operating an illegal pyramid selling scheme which brought in more than 3.2 billion yuan ($250 million) from local governments and businesses before collapsing.

According to intelligence officials who monitor China, corruption allegations were even directed at Premier Li Peng himself. Peng was vulnerable to the investigations, largely because of the suspicious business activities of his wife and son - who is a vice-president of a company with a subsidiary listed on the New York Stock Exchange.

It is this high level of corruption across the border which so worries the people and police of Hong Kong, only just returned to the 'mother country'. It was a problem in the surrounding areas of the Pearl River delta even before the establishment of Hong Kong because of the illegal opium trade and now a booming local economy is providing further encouragement to cut corners.

China's influence has been a constant presence. In 1967 the Cultural Revolution spilled over into Hong Kong, resulting in serious civil unrest. As police attention was drawn towards maintaining public order, other problems such as narcotics, prostitution, hawking and gambling proliferated. Corrupt police officers and officials capitalised upon the situation and dishonesty grew to an unprecedented and unacceptable level. The Anti Corruption office of the Royal Hong Kong Police had little success in its drive against bribery, despite the introduction of new legislation creating heavier penalties and new offences in 1972. Then, in June 1973, Peter Godber, a Hong Kong police Chief Superintendent, fled the colony while under investigation for having assets disproportionate to his income. The incident created an uproar in the community and there were calls for the creation of an independent body to address the problem. A Commission of Inquiry was established under a Senior Judge, Sir Alistair Blair-Kerr, which looked into the circumstances of Godber's flight, examined the effectiveness of the anti-corruption laws, and suggested amendments. Following the publication of the report, the Governor, Sir Murray (later Lord) MacLehose, announced a new body; an Independent Commission Against Corruption (ICAC) would be formed to combat corruption within the colony.

It was soon realised that the first task for this new organisation would be to get Godber back to Hong Kong. After a legal battle, Godber was extradited to Hong Kong from the United Kingdom and convicted on two charges of bribery. He was sentenced to four years imprisonment.

SINCE that initial success, the ICAC has gone from strength to strength, delivering the three pronged attack upon corruption it has adopted: investigation, within a strong legal framework; prevention; and education - to change attitudes.

The ICAC's teeth lie in the Prevention of Bribery Ordinance, which contains a number of powerful investigative tools and offences: of being or having been a public servant maintaining a standard of living or controlling assets disproportionate to past or present emoluments; disclosing the identity of a person under investigation or details of such an investigation; making false report of the commission of offences; and misleading investigating officers. ICAC officers have powers to inspect and demand the production of accounts and documents; to require suspects to provide information and to give details of their assets; to enter and search premises for evidence; to restrict the disposal of property; and to require the surrender of travel documents by persons under investigation.

The level of funding given to the Commission is impressive, but it remains to be seen whether China will maintain its work. The Operations Department has over 800 staff, 140 of whom are involved in surveillance functions. Such high staffing levels send a powerful message to the public, and more importantly to those tempted to turn to corruption.

The ICAC is probably the best anti-corruption unit in the world. It has long recognised the consensual and secretive ways of the corrupt and, to this end, its techniques focus upon what it describes as 'breaking-open clamshells' by the use of physical and technical surveillance, undercover operations, informants, or whistleblowers, and special reporting procedures.

Physical surveillance is used to great effect and there is emphasis upon 'real time' investigations as opposed to working with historical material and attempting to reconstruct events. Many ICAC officers have told me they would not even entertain an investigation which depended upon historical material because they feel a great need to be party to actual events through surveillance, from both audio and visual devices.

One senior officer I met during my time studying the ICAC described his job as 'playing enormous practical jokes upon criminals'. This was his way of introducing me to the use of undercover operations to infiltrate suspect groups. The high cost of such operations is borne as being a very effective way of rooting out corruption from the inside.

Like other forces around the world the ICAC uses informants from the criminal fraternity. Provision can be made for convicted informants to serve part of their sentence in secure 'flatlets' in the Detention Centre, where they are safe from retribution and available for in-depth debriefings by officers to provide further intelligence on corruption in the colony.

But one reason for the success of the ICAC is the way they have ingrained their work into the minds of the public. One of the best means of making corruption a common thought in the minds of the law-abiding community is by publicising both the individual offences and the investigative work undertaken by the ICAC.

Emphasis is placed upon making the reporting of corruption simple but effective. A 'Report Centre' with a 'hot-line' telephone number is manned round the clock every single day of the year to receive reports of corruption from the public. The number is well-publicised and, judging by the more than 7,000 reports and queries it receives annually, it is well used. Supporting the aim of making the reporting of corruption easier, the organisation operates eight regional offices which take the Commission to the door-steps of various local community groups as well as serving as centres for receiving complaints and enquiries about corruption.

THE ICAC also employs approximately 60 personnel to work in corruption prevention. This department advises government agencies on improvements to procedures and practices, examines the operations of public sector management systems (and then recommends changes to reduce corruption opportunities) and increases the corruption awareness of public officials through seminars, conferences and publications.

The organisation realises that an element of pragmatism has to be built into such assignments and solutions must be realistic. Their task is to find methods by which work can be carried out with maximum efficiency while reducing the opportunities for corruption to a minimum. In this, they must achieve a delicate balance.

Corruption Prevention officers are told upon appointment that the simplest way to eliminate corruption is to encourage good management. A strategy targeting policy makers and managers gives their department a lever with which to influence behaviour disproportionate to the number of officers employed. Persuasive arguments aimed at awakening managers to their duty are reinforced by building into prevention strategies systems of accountability. There are points where pressure may be applied to good preventative effect. An accountable system, under which people are responsible for the acts or omissions of those they supervise, is recognised as a valuable tool. The Corruption Prevention staff includes officers with a wide range of experience, including former police officers and seconded government servants. Within the organisation there is a willingness to hire outside expertise in a particular field, should it be required.

The ingenuity displayed by prevention staff in Hong Kong to get to the root of a problem would surprise many. The use of satellite surveillance to monitor the illegal dumping of waste at sea is just one example.

THERE IS little doubt the founding of the ICAC in 1974 was a declaration of all out war on corruption, and as part of that battle a huge campaign was launched for the 'hearts and minds' of the public. The Community Relations Department aims to educate the Hong Kong public against the evils of corruption and to harness public support for ICAC programmes. Some 200 staff are allocated to the role.

The strategies used may have some roots in the previous counter-insurgency experience of some of the founding members of the ICAC. The broad message is that corruption hurts everyone in a community; that everyone somehow suffers in paying the price of bribery.

To get their message across, the ICAC conducts multi-media campaigns to inform the community about the problems associated with corruption and to encourage its reporting. Uniquely, television advertisements have been running from the mid-1970s including short television clips carrying subtle psychological messages and playing upon cultural traits. For example, bent businessmen are often shown as crocodiles, which is an animal

reviled in Chinese folklore. Similarly, emphasis is placed upon the shame felt by families of the corrupt, as the loss of face in the community carries great stigma in Chinese culture.

In the late 1970s the Hong Kong ICAC produced a series of professional television programmes with an anti-corruption theme. One series, depicting ICAC investigators at work, was an enormous

Hong Kong must be one of the few countries in the world to have a popular anti-corruption gameshow, seen here in this video still.

success and it is now produced by a private television production company. Such programmes not only keep the public informed of the work of the Commission, but also show the evils of corruption and help to cultivate a sense of social responsibility. Television campaigns are almost invariably supported by poster campaigns pursuing the same theme. Both media carry the same message, - corruption is anti social and should be reported.

No efforts are spared to remove any barrier to the making of complaints and the regional offices handle approximately 1,200 reports and 3,500 enquiries each year.

The organisation also goes after youngsters. About 20% of Hong Kong's population are students, from primary school pupils to university undergraduates, and all are targeted by the Community Relations Department. Children in primary schools, too young to grasp the concept of corruption, are given a basic grounding in ethics: the importance of honesty, the difference between right and wrong. When students reach secondary school they begin to formally study corruption. The ICAC is discussed in the overall context of law and order and the subject of corruption is dealt with alongside other social evils such as highly dangerous triad societies and drug trafficking.

As the children become adults, the ICAC continues to ram home its message, contributing to seminars, conferences, workshops and training meetings for public sector employees. During 1994, it gave talks to 11,079 civil servants as part of their induction or refresher training. They also produce comprehensive guides for senior civil servants to help them promote staff integrity.

In 1993 the last British Governor of Hong Kong, Chris Patten, announced in his policy address the launch of a "Campaign on Business Ethics', the objective being to enhance Hong Kong's commercial ethics and preserve the territory's image as a major international business centre.

The campaign began with a conference held in May 1994 organised by the ICAC with six major Chambers of Commerce and sponsored by 108 trade and professional associations. It was an important recognition that it is of long term strategic importance for Hong Kong to promote and sustain a high level of business ethical standards.

Since then, advice and support in the wording of corporate codes of conduct has been given to many listed and large private companies as well as chambers and trade associations in Hong Kong. Smaller companies are assisted through a Business Ethics Participation Project, whereby trade associations and professional bodies design their own education activities on business ethics and corruption prevention for transmission to their member companies, with the ICAC providing small subsidies and technical guidance. As a focal point, the Ethics Development Centre requested by the Conference on Business Ethics has now been established in the Wan Chai district of Hong Kong. By mid-1995, more than 1,200 publicly listed or large private companies and trade associations had adopted a corporate code of conduct.

Power and Corruption

A CHIEF Investigator of the Hong Kong ICAC told me: "Corruption is a secret act and to combat it requires draconian powers". Together with many other people, I would agree with this statement, but concern arises if such power was to go unbridled. For this reason the Commission is subject to checks and balances to ensure its proper operation.

Every aspect of the ICAC comes under the scrutiny of independent committees comprising responsible citizens drawn from all sectors of the community. For example, the Advisory Committee on Corruption reviews the overall policy of the Commission, and should any aspect of the ICAC's organisation or operation cause concern to the Committee, its terms of reference require it to draw such problems to the attention of the politicians.

The ICAC's three-pronged strategy to wage war on corruption has been used to great effect, which begs the question: what are the factors which indicate corruption in Hong Kong is under control? Perhaps some statistics can help. In the early years of the ICAC, over 80% of corruption reports related to the public sector. In 1994, less than 50% of reports did so. In 1974, 45% of corruption reports concerned the police. In 1994, by comparison, that figure was down to 18%. In the first ICAC public opinion survey conducted in 1977, 38% of the people surveyed thought corruption was widespread in government departments. In 1994, only 7.8% thought this was so.

In the 1994 public opinion survey, only 2.9% of the people surveyed said they would tolerate corruption. During 1994 71% of people reporting corruption were prepared to identify themselves, as opposed to 33% in 1974, which indicates excellent public confidence in the organisation.

THE YEARS before the handover of Hong Kong to China in July 1997 saw a dramatic upsurge in corruption, however, even among the police, as everyone tried to make their fortunes before the heavy hand of China clamped-down. The ICAC's Business Ethics Campaign still has a difficult task. Bertrand de Speville, the former ICAC Commissioner, said a number of 'small syndicates' of corrupt officers had been discovered and broken up, although there are almost certainly other groups. More than 80 ICAC officers were deployed amid evidence of concerted attempts to win influence with officials with pro-China leanings. "What we are seeing in these organised groups, in the way they operate, is very reminiscent of the bad old days," the Commissioner added.

The police and civil service were particularly susceptible, he said, because people want to make money as quickly as possible. "This is true in the civil service generally, but the police have a particular problem."

During the dying days of empire, at least 153 officers were under investigation, including a superintendent, 25 sergeants and seven top-ranking inspectors. Some of the officers were suspected of receiving bribes 'to lay-off' organised criminals, gambling and prostitution. Others were facing prosecution for involvement in armed robbery.

There were mutterings that a perceived delay in bringing suspects to justice was to avoid public panic over the sheer numbers of corrupt officers. "The ICAC is walking on egg-shells," said one insider. According to long-serving members of staff the atmosphere was reminiscent of the days when the ICAC was first established. In that era, dozens of police officers were arrested for corruption; the police held mass meetings and then responded by storming the ICAC offices and beating up the staff.

So what happens now? "The public will no longer accept police corruption. The police close ranks and they're much smarter. No officer is going to walk around the way he used to, bragging about his take and waving bundles of notes," said the insider. Many independent experts have said that although the ICAC is successfully catching many corrupt businessmen and police officers, crime in Hong Kong is so sophisticated even the ICAC is not capable of defeating it. However there is little doubt the ICAC's successes have attracted great public and international attention.

Shortly before he left, Chris Patten, the last Governor of the colony, proudly said corruption had been driven to the margins of Hong Kong's public and commercial life. Even now that the territory has been handed over to China, the ICAC still carries a very large investigative stick.

Chapter Fifteen

THE JURY
IS OUT

"So little done, so much to do"
Cecil Rhodes

C ORRUPTION in the Third World leads to the distortion of economies and the diversion of funds from health and education programmes. It also scares off foreign investment - thereby preventing the formulation of a mobilised, educated population that is eager to participate in the democratic process.

Sleaze in Western democracies is just as damaging because it undermines public confidence in the political process. This in turn leads to a lack of participation in democratic decision-making and a concentration of power in the hands of ever fewer politicians. In turn this creates opportunities for further misconduct - a spiral of decline.

Re-establishing public confidence is in any event a monumental task. Bribery or undue influence may have allowed someone to profit from an arrangement, but it may be well nigh impossible to prove and then prosecute the culprit for lack of hard evidence.

Alternatively, there may be smoke but no fire - with people suspecting that some deal is unfair when, if all the facts were known, it is above-board. In between these two extremes is sleaze: behaviour by public officials that is not illegal but which is questionable and, in the public's opinion, undesirable. In each case, the preferred answer is prevention because, sadly, the alternatives are so hit and miss.

Even in those instances when hard evidence is available, the system of justice in Britain is stacked in favour of the defendant. On this I can draw upon my own experiences in investigating and prosecuting public sector corruption and major fraud, and highlight a number of key areas for reform.

While I have the greatest respect for the jury system for most types of case, I do not believe the interests of justice are served by retaining juries for fraud and corruption trials, where the possibility that a jury will be confused is immense. The art of prosecuting any criminal case lies in keeping the case as simple as possible for presentation to a jury. Conversely, on many occasions the best way to defend the accused in a fraud or corruption trial is to make the matter as complicated as possible.

The nature of fraud and corruption investigations, certainly at the higher end of the scale, almost invariably means there are large

Thank you! You know, that I would never dream of accepting if I didn't know that the phenomenon was global.

Laxman, Times of India

A witty comment from India.

amounts of documentary material which the prosecution aims to slim down to what is essential to prove a case. Meanwhile the defence lawyers are hoping to introduce ever more evidence and documentation to confuse, and even bore or fatigue the jury.

One sees a hasty change of tactics by the defence if the prosecution seeks to introduce detailed evidence to prove a regular pattern, or a system of fraudulent and corrupt behaviour. If successful, this destroys the defence argument that illegality on one particular occasion was a single mistake. At times like this, I am no longer surprised at the number of defence counsel who gently warn the judge that introducing more evidence will lengthen the trial. They know judges are under constant pressure to minimise the duration of cases to avoid forcing juries to consider evidence they heard months previously.

Trial judges inform juries that interpretation of the law is a matter for the judge whereas interpretation of the facts is their preserve. Most jurors will have experienced the gamut of emotions which surround offences of violence, and may have been the victims of theft or burglary. They would have no problem following the evidence of a rape trial but I have personally witnessed a number of jurors in fraud trials struggling to read the oath when being sworn in.

How can they then be expected to understand or follow the financial intricacies of a complicated corruption case? At such times, justice becomes merely a lottery for the prosecution and the defence.

In 1986 the Fraud Trials Committee, chaired by Lord Roskill, recommended juries should be abandoned in cases of fraud and replaced by expert tribunals. Juries, it was argued, cannot have a proper grasp of banking, legal or local governmental procedures. The proposal was never adopted but the debate still rages on - as it should.

THERE ARE other reasons to prefer prevention rather than prosecution, specifically the difficulties of obtaining evidence from overseas, the vast costs of mounting prosecutions and the logistical nightmares created by the storage and cataloguing of tonnes of paper exhibits.

However there are clearly many occasions when prosecution is necessary, and at such times the investigator strives to conduct a thorough and professional investigation to present the best case possible to the court.

In presenting such a case my advice to anybody in a similar situation would be to collect as much 'real time' evidence as possible. When corruption is suspected, it is far better to identify the players, and utilise surveillance techniques, undercover officers, 'stings' and telephone intercepts to monitor the criminal conspiracy as it unfolds.

There will come a stage when premises will need to be raided and documents seized but at that point the criminals will be aware they need to cover their tracks. Producing a case based largely on historical, documentary evidence to a court is much more difficult, particularly if several years have elapsed since the crimes took place and memories have faded.

There is a problem in Britain in using telephone intercept transcripts in evidence. However, it is now much more difficult to doctor such evidence, and technical analysis can detect if a tape has been edited. Prevented from using this evidence, the police are shackled. They may know beyond all doubt that a crime has taken place but forced to exclude the most compelling evidence available. It is an enormous frustration to all the detectives I work with.

Some argue that using such surveillance methods tends to become counter-productive - along the lines of 'once the criminals realise we can listen, they will not use the telephone'. This is a complete fallacy, as my own studies in Australia confirmed. Newspapers there frequently carry stories of criminals convicted by the evidence of telephone intercepts, yet the harvest of criminals continues. In Britain every 'good' criminal already works on the premise that his or her phone calls are monitored, which of course they are not. The current rules handicap the police in their battle with criminals, and new legislation needs to be introduced.

IT IS HEARTENING to hear the Law Commission is seeking to reform the law in relation to corruption and is seeking opinions on the shape of future legislation. Current proposals are to simplify the major pieces of anti-corruption legislation into one modern statute to cover both the public and private sectors, with the focus of the offences being upon those exercising discretion on behalf of others. The new statute will encompass offences committed by judges, local councillors, police officers and - as agents of the public - all those who have undertaken to discharge a public duty whether appointed as public office holders, or to perform a specified public function. MPs will also be subject to any new legislation.

Apart from problems referred to earlier making the prosecution of MPs for bribery very difficult, the present law in relation to corruption in Britain suffers from numerous defects. It is drawn from many sources, at least 11 statutes containing anti-corruption provisions. The principal offences are contained within the Prevention of Corruption Acts 1889 to 1916, which apply - with small differences - in Scotland as well as England and Wales. Though referred to as the Prevention of Corruption Acts 1889 to 1916, the legislation was enacted in three distinct phases.

The 1889 Public Bodies Corrupt Practices Act was introduced following revelations of malpractice connected with property development. It was originally only concerned with local public bodies in the United Kingdom. The 1906 Prevention of Corruption Act extended the law of corruption to all agents, including those in the private sector, but it is uncertain as to whether certain post holders, such as judges, fall within the definition of agent. Another problem with the act is that it does not cover bribes offered to or accepted by an agent in the immediate period before and after they hold their position; for example, bribes offered to an individual to approve a certain contract just before they start a new job in a company as contracts manager.

The 1916 Prevention of Corruption Act was the result of wartime scandals involving War Office contracts. The legislation increased the maximum sentence for bribery in relation to contracts with the government or public bodies, widened the definition of 'public body' given in the 1889 Act and introduced a 'presumption of corruption' under certain circumstances. The presumption created a reversal of the burden of proof making it a matter for the defence to prove, on the balance of probabilities, that a payment was not corrupt. The presumption, however, applies only to payments made to employees of public bodies and not elected officials and applies only to contracts, but not 'permissions' such as the granting of planning permission.

Apart from the statutory offences under the Prevention of Corruption Acts 1889-1916 there are common law offences of bribery and misconduct in public office. These offences are not easily defined and often overlap with the statutory offences.

In short, the legislation in the United Kingdom presents a number of difficulties. It is confused, lacks consistency and is not comprehensive. Many slip through the net because of gaps in the legislation. There is now even more confusion as to what comprises a public body following privatisation programmes and the supply of public services by private concerns.

What must be considered by those drafting any modern statute is the inclusion of provisions to break open the clamshell that is corruption.

IRONICALLY there have been plenty of opportunities to reform the law, most notably after the Poulson scandal of the 1970s. Two reports following the arrest of local authority officials and members - Redcliffe-Maud and the Salmon Report suggested ways of tightening the law and, in the light of the widespread nature of Poulson's bribery to win contracts one would have thought they would pass smoothly through the Parliamentary process. Not only did this not happen, the findings of the report were barely debated by our MPs.

The reports pointed up the fact that no laws can adequately police all wrong-doing and highlighted the importance of the press in publicising questionable behaviour by public officials. This is in theory a nice idea, and the press do attempt to act as a public watchdog but the evidence shows that fewer and fewer local newspapers have the resources to tackle such enquiries and the British libel laws ac as a severe restriction. Indeed a newspaper probably needs enough evidence to convict someone of corruption before it can safely expose it.

The lack of post-Poulson debate in Parliament reflects one important feature of how the British public regard corruption. They do not believe it is a problem. The truth they barely see the top of the iceberg as any serving police officer like myself can testify. Britain is not an island of probity, as the public seem to think.

Because of this, and after much consideration, I would urge powers be given to the police similar in nature to those coercive powers possessed by the Serious Fraud Office (SFO) as a result of the Criminal Justice Act 1987. The SFO can compel, under threat of penalty, the provision of answers to questions, and require the production of documents. They can also search for and seize documents. Claims of banking confidentiality should not be allowed, while legal claims of professional privilege should be preserved in the interests of justice. Similar sufficient safeguards to those contained within the Criminal Justice Act 1987 would protect against 'self-incrimination'.

LEGISLATION must also be enacted to require relevant government bodies, in particular Her Majesty's Customs and Excise and the Inland Revenue, to render all assistance and to furnish information to the investigating police officers. It may surprise outsiders to know that during investigation of serious corruption allegations, taxation records will not be made available to police officers as a matter of course.

The legislation must also recognise instances where no misconduct is provable but benefit is traced to the public official or alternatively no benefit is actually traced to the official, but there is evidence of misconduct. One of the most powerful weapons used in Hong Kong against corruption should also be adopted in Britain. Section 10(1) of their Prevention of Bribery Ordinance 1970 states that: "Any person who, being or having been a Crown Servant, maintains a standard of living above that which is commensurate with his present or past official emolument; or is in control of pecuniary resources or property disproportionate to his present or past official emolument - shall, unless he gives a satisfactory explanation to the court as to how he was able to maintain such a standard of living, or how such pecuniary resources or property came under his control, be guilty of an offence."

As we have already discussed, it is one of the biggest weapons in the Hong Kong ICAC's armoury. The law was intended to capture those officials who were clearly accepting bribes in their official capacity, but who could not be prosecuted due to the consensual nature of the crime. One wonders how many more civil servants like Foxley and Allcock (both corrupt officials mentioned earlier) are escaping prosecution for lack of evidence, while their lifestyles are clearly disproportionate to their official salaries.

However, anybody with a knowledge of the European Convention on Human Rights will, by this point, know these proposals will face a challenge. Though the Convention has not yet been incorporated into English domestic law, British citizens have a right to petition the Strasbourg Commission and - if the petition is allowed - to pursue the matter at the European Court of Human Rights.

It is not necessary to look further than the crucial passages of the Convention which state that everyone charged with a criminal offence is entitled to a fair public hearing and shall be presumed innocent until proven guilty according to law.

But I am not suggesting that information gleaned under compulsion during a corruption investigation should be admissible against the provider of that evidence during their trial. Information collected by the British Serious Fraud Office under similar circumstances is not admissible except under very special circumstances. Such information would, however, provide valuable intelligence - at the very least - to allow further admissible evidence to be sought elsewhere.

What about reversing the burden of proof and forcing a suspect public servant to explain his or her apparent wealth? In other words, placing the onus on them to prove their innocence. The Strasbourg Court has previously opposed this suggestion. But what does an innocent man have to fear?

The problem in instituting such legislation in the United Kingdom would lie in dealing with Strasbourg's insistence on "reasonable limits" and "the importance of what is at stake". Here again we confront the argument of the ignorant that such a law, with some watering down of a defendant's rights, can be justified in places such as Hong Kong because of their level of corruption, but not in the Europe because we don't have a serious problem. This is simply untrue. We must work to prevent and deter corruption, not merely respond piecemeal after the event.

Legislation similar to Section 10(1) would be a valuable weapon worth fighting for at Strasbourg, if the scale of the problem was more widely acknowledged. Only then will investigators be given the tools to confront, for example, police officers corrupted by organised crime - of which we in Britain have so far only begun to see the tip of a much larger national problem.

WHAT OF the situation referred to earlier, where there is evidence of misconduct on the part of a public official, but no proof they have received any benefit? Prosecutions have previously been mounted under the common law for the offence of misbehaviour in a public office, most recently R v Bowden in 1995, where a maintenance officer of a City Council caused unnecessary works to be undertaken by council employees at the premises of a friend.

While this prosecution was successful, it was challenged by the defence on the grounds that the circumstances did not apply to the law as stated. The prosecution smacked of making the law fit the circumstance, a far from ideal situation. I also have experience of 'conspiracy to defraud' charges being laid at the end of investigations, where if we could have proved that actual benefits were given, the proper charges would have been under anti-corruption legislation. Thought should be given to legislation which would capture public figures - employees or elected officials - who further the interests of family, friends and associates where no benefit can be shown to have been passed to the public official in return. Such legislation should also address the problem of sensitive information being leaked from public bodies to allow some to benefit at the expense of others, including the public body, which is thereby put at a disadvantage by a breach of trust.

But what of prevention? In considering any preventative measures, basic premises are paramount: corruption takes place in the shadows, and the dark breeds conspiracy theories as much as it breeds corruption. Therein lies the key to the prevention of both corruption and perceived corruption. A brighter light needs to be shone on public affairs and the actions of those in the public service.

189

One great leap forward would be the loosening of the laws of libel in the United Kingdom requiring public figures to display a degree of resilience in the face of criticism and justified press comment. In addition, a Freedom of Information Act would result in better informed public debate and a commitment to transparency in public life, while legislation to protect whistleblowers would complete the assault on secrecy and dark practices.

I also believe the electorate has a right to know who is bankrolling political parties and judge for itself whether any favours are being sought as a result. Certainly the publication of lists of political donors donating in excess of £5,000 would allow the electorate to draw its own inferences if any were seen to be beneficiaries from any policy change.

I see no merit in the argument for state funding of political parties, because those enjoying little public support would become financially dependent on the taxpayer. However I believe placing limits on the amount of money which can be spent during an election campaign would lead to a levelling of the playing-field. Foreign donations should be banned, for no other reason than excessive donations can be more easily disguised by transmitting a number of smaller amounts from overseas, using aliases or front men. For this same reason, no donations should be allowed from offshore accounts held by UK nationals, because of the inherent difficulties in tracing such donations to their true sources.

ONCE they have succeeded in convincing enough of the electorate that they are the right people to represent their constituents at Westminster, MPs need to realise that together with political power goes accountability. With accountability should go a degree of openness and a recognition that the electorate have a right to formulate considered judgements.

An MP is required to register an interest if services are provided in his or her capacity as an MP, but at present there are too many loopholes which permit only partial disclosure. All interests and benefits should be disclosed in the interests of transparency and the maintenance of public confidence. Those who would rather not disclose have an obvious course of action - choose another career.

Lobbyists and Quango members also require oversight in the interests of a clean political environment. The voluntary register of lobbyists deposited with the House of Commons, which lists firms, consultants and clients, must be given the force of law, with compulsory registration for all lobbyists, a right of public inspection, and a right of access by a nominee of Parliament to business records of lobbyists. Membership lists of all Quangos showing names, addresses, remuneration, period of office and political and pecuniary interests should also be publicly available.

Should those pursuing a career in public service also choose to follow the craft of Freemasonry or another secret society, they should be prepared to disclose membership as proposed for police officers by the Association of Chief Police Officers. Unwarranted secrecy and potential conflicts of interest, whether they are real or simply perceived have no place in the public service.

In a similar vein, guidance, already provided in some sectors, should be given to all public servants as to how to best avoid potential conflicts of interest during the course of employment and how to properly disclose interests or benefits to avoid suspicion falling upon them. The Hong Kong model code would be of great assistance in this matter.

ASIDE from the principles of transparency and openness already advocated, supervision is crucial to ensure proper procedures are followed. It is a nonsense that European Auditors can trace European Union funds expended in the United Kingdom, but the National Audit Office, along with the Comptroller and Auditor General of the United Kingdom, Sir John Bourn, do not hold similar powers in relation to private companies providing public services.

'Supervision' should be a watchword in the fight against corruption in law enforcement, procurement, the granting of concessions and regulatory functions. Proper controls linked to awareness of the threat, danger signs and integrity checks, will go a long way to deterring misconduct.

It has already been argued that the battle against international corruption, with all the attendant damage it causes, needs to be fought on the supranational level by organisations such as the OECD, OAS, the World Bank, the World Trade Organisation and Transparency International. In their efforts, I wish them well and much luck, especially in overcoming the questionable strategies of the world's armaments industries.

The United Kingdom now stands on the threshold of a great opportunity to rid itself of the sleazy image which haunted the final years of the Conservative government (defeated by the Labour Party at the general election of May 1997). I would urge the new government to seize the opportunity with both hands and make radical reforms to ensure transparency in public life.

Should the challenge fail to be met, I fear a time will come when the electorate compares standards under Labour with those under the Conservatives. An image from George Orwell's Animal Farm comes to mind, with the public looking through the window of a farmhouse at the political creatures inside: They "looked from pig to man and from man to pig and from pig to man again; but already it was impossible to say which was which."

Index

About VISION:

VISION was founded by the former Chief Investigative Reporter of The Sunday Times of London, and comprises a group of investigative newspaper and television journalists from Britain and North America working for VISION Paperbacks, VISION Investigations and VISION TV Productions.

By combining the skills of a group of experienced international writers with leading academics and experts, Vision is publishing books for an international audience on subjects in the news or that make the news.

The topics we chose for investigation are truly global issues. Many current-affairs books contain acres of boring newsprint; in contrast Vision books are written in a lively style and are designed to appeal to a wide audience.

Other books from VISION Paperbacks:

THE MILLENNIUM BOMB - Countdown to a £400bn Catastrophe

by Simon Reeve and Colin McGhee

This is the first book in the world to investigate the so-called Year 2000 problem, whereby millions of computers across the globe will go haywire in just a few years simply because they cannot cope with the change of date.

For decades, computer technicians have been using two digits to represent the year, forgetting that computers will think the year 2000 is the year 1900. The authors, two investigative journalists, show how this could cause chaos. Party-goers could be stuck in lifts, missile defence systems could shut down, and stock market trading systems could fail. Almost anything electronic is at risk and companies will inevitably collapse. This is the story of a $600 billion catastrophe - one of mankind's most expensive mistakes. The topic - mixing as it does many people's fear of technology with a real millennium disaster - is a fascinating subject.

£8.99   ISBN: 1 901250 00 8

INSTRUMENTS OF TERROR - Mass Destruction has never been so easy . . .

by Dr Frank Barnaby

Terrorism has become an unstoppable threat and it is only a matter of time before a renegade group detonates a weapon of mass destruction, warns Dr Frank Barnaby, an internationally respected defence analyst, in this investigative book.

With information gleaned from intelligence sources, Dr Barnaby warns that terrorism has become an unstoppable threat from terrorists with no moral restrictions on mass killing, and he investigates how states such as Iraq are engaged in a world-wide race with government secret agents to acquire their own crude atomic weapons.

Dr Barnaby also warns of the threat of 'cyber-terrorism': weapons which destroy a nation's infrastructure by attacking crucial computers.

Professor Barnaby is the former head of the Stockholm International Peace Research Institute and also relates in the book how he travelled into the Colombian jungle to help disarm a ruthless terrorist group.

£8.99   ISBN: 1 901250 01 6

GANGSTA - The Sinister Spread of Yardie Gun Culture

by John Davison

A man intervenes in a row at an illegal drinking den. He is shot and left for dead.
A woman argues with a crack dealer. She is marched at gun-point up three flights of stairs, beaten over the head and thrown out of a window.

These are not scenes from a television cop show but the reality of life among the 'Yardie' criminals who have exploded out of Jamaica across the West. These 'Gangstas' live in a world where the gun means power.

After spending months researching this book, John Davison, an award-winning investigative journalists, gained unprecedented access to gangstas, ghettos and undercover police operations. He graphically describes shoot-outs, bungled police raids and tells an amazing story of gang violence.

£8.99   ISBN: 1 901250 02 4

BIOWAR - The Secrets of Test-Tube Weapons

by Wendy Barnaby

Frightening new evidence shows how genetic engineering and other biological advances are helping to create terrifying new 'invisible' weapons, capable of killing millions of people. Biowar reveals who is behind these programmes - including scientists who do not realise their research is being used by the military.

Biowar explains how it may be possible to target specific types of people or particular ethnic groups. There are few safeguards and, in contrast to nuclear weapons, the public has not been fully alerted to the dangers. After reading this book there can be no excuse for ignorance. Several countries have now admitted they have secret germ warfare programmes, while Iraq has used them, and South Africa has been perfecting biowarfare for 'offensive purposes'.

But equally worrying is the ease with which cults and terrorist groups could cause mayhem. Biowar reveals how Iraq has developed thousands of tons of bio-weapons and examines the risks of these weapons being passed to terrorists. The book also warns that individuals can manufacture their own crude Bio-weapons. Little wonder when their manufacture is: "about as complicated as manufacturing beer and less dangerous then refining heroin".

£9.99   ISBN: 1 901250 04 0

LAWYERS - ON THE SPOT

Donna Leigh-Kile and Rhoda Koenig

Love them or loathe them, everyone has an opinion on lawyers. Are they over-paid and under-principled? Why are they so secretive? Do they really deserve some of the highest professional salaries? The lid is taken off the high-flyers in the legal profession, with controversial results. The authors show why it takes more than talent to get to the top. Tough tactics and media exploitation have become accepted practice to beat the competition. Greed, dishonesty, apathy and even power-mania are exposed - as are people genuinely battling for justice. The curious and envious will be fascinated and amused; because this is not just a serious examination of the world of top lawyers.

£9.99   ISBN: 1 901250 06 7

WOMAN FROM MOSSAD - The Torment of Mordechai Vanunu
by Peter Hounam

Mordechai Vanunu, who divulged to a newspaper the secrets of Israel's clandestine nuclear weapons programme suffered a terrible fate after he met a beautiful blonde American woman called Cindy in the heart of London. Before his remarkable story could be published by The Sunday Times, Cindy had lured him to Rome with the promise of sex. Having fallen into a classic honey trap, he was attacked by agents from Mossad, Israel's spy network, drugged and smuggled back home to stand trial for treason.

This new book brings the Vanunu saga right up to date with new and disturbing revelations about the kidnap, the story of Cindy, and how her spying days were numbered when she was identified and exposed by the author. Peter Hounam was the journalist who first befriended Vanunu and helped him tell the world the full extent of Israel's guilty nuclear secrets. His book shows how Israel received secret foreign help from Western powers. It is a gripping adventure story that takes the reader across three continents. It is also a story of international intrigue and human tragedy.

£9.99   ISBN: 1 901250 05 9

ALL VISION BOOKS ARE AVAILABLE FROM YOUR LOCAL BOOKSHOP OR THROUGH OUR MAIL ORDER HOTLINE - TBS DIRECT: 01621 819 596

**VISION
20 Queen Anne Street
London
W1M 0AY
Tel: +44 (0)171 323 9757
Fax: +44 (0)171 323 9747**